CULTURES OF THE WORLD

CHINA

Peggy Ferroa/Elaine Chan

BENCHMARK BOOKS

MARSHALL CAVENDISH
NEW YORK

PICTURE CREDITS
Cover photo: © Trip/A. Tovy
Liz Berryman: 3, 6, 37, 38, 62, 69, 85, 106, 107, 115, 119, 120 • Bes Stock: title, 12, 14
• Peggy Ferroa: 31, 65 • Getty Images/Hulton Archive: 43, 44, 45, 46, 47, 49 • Graham
Uden Photography: 80, 100 • Jimmy Kang: 35, 39 • Chapman Lee: 26, 30, 67, 74, 78, 81,
94, 95, 99, 114, 127, 129 • Life File Photo Library: 4, 20, 58, 120, 121 • Lawrence Lim: 71
(bottom) • Lonely Planet Images: 80, 130, 131 • Photobank: 5, 36 • Bernard Sonneville:
11, 18, 23, 25, 27, 29, 32, 40, 41, 43, 51, 59, 64, 71 (top), 75, 82, 92, 93, 96 (top right), 102,
105, 116, 118, 124 • Ed Stokes: 104 • Topham Picturepoint: 16, 42, 50 • Trip Photographic
Library: 57 • Wang Miao: 8, 9, 10, 13, 15, 28, 34, 46, 47, 54, 55, 63, 66, 68, 76, 77, 83, 88,
89, 90, 97, 101, 108, 110, 112, 113, 122, 125, 128 • Xinhua News Agency: 60, 70, 124
• Yim Chee Peng: 126

ACKNOWLEDGMENTS
With thanks to Dr. Cui Zhiyuan, East Asian Institute, National University of Singapore,
for his expert reading of this manuscript.

PRECEDING PAGE
Two Chinese schoolgirls share a park bench.

Marshall Cavendish Corporation
99 White Plains Road
Tarrytown, NY 10591
Website: www.marshallcavendish.us

Originated and designed by Times Books International
An imprint of Marshall Cavendish International (Asia) Private Limited
A member of Times Publishing Limited

Library of Congress Cataloging-in-Publication Data
Ferroa, Peggy Grace, 1959–
    China / by Peggy Ferroa.—2nd ed.
        p. cm.—(Cultures of the world)
    Summary: Presents the history, geography, government, economy, environment,
        religion, people, and social life and customs of China.
    Includes bibliographical references and index.
    ISBN 0-7614-1474-6
    1. China—Juvenile literature. I. Title. II. Series.
DS706.F38 2002
951—dc21   2002019209

Printed in China

7 6 5

CONTENTS

Playing elephant chess, a favorite pastime among the Chinese.

Women in China work side by side with men in the fields, in government, and in large organizations.

INTRODUCTION

CHINA WAS HOME to one of the most ancient civilizations in the world. The country has 5,000 years of history filled with wars and political turbulence. China's silk, tea, and spices attracted the interest of the West, and traders traveled to China overland across Europe along the Silk Road.

In 1949, after a bloody civil war, China became the People's Republic of China under Communist rule led by Mao Zedong. In the years that followed, the country isolated itself from the outside world until Mao's death in 1976.

Economic reforms introduced in 1978 by Mao's successor, Deng Xiaoping, opened the door to foreign investors and put China back on the world stage. The reforms introduced free market principles and spurred phenomenal economic growth.

GEOGRAPHY

THE MIDDLE KINGDOM, as China is known to the Chinese, sits in East Asia and covers an area of 3.7 million square miles (9.6 million square km). Geographically it is the third largest country in the world, slightly larger than the United States of America. China spans 3,100 miles (4,989 km) from east to west and 4,320 miles (6,952 km) from north to south.

China borders 15 countries. The 8,700-mile (14,000-km) coastline touches the Bohai, Yellow, East, and South China seas. China has more than 5,000 islands—of which Taiwan is the largest—in its territorial seas.

Below: **China and its neighbors.**

Opposite: **A hillside farming village.**

MOUNTAINOUS TERRAIN

China's land mass consists mainly of mountains, plateaus, and deserts. Of the total land mass, only 13.5 percent can be used for agriculture to feed 1.3 billion people. It is, therefore, a feat that China grows enough food to feed its own people and to export to other countries. In the southwest is the Tibetan plateau, the world's highest at 13,500 feet (4,115 m). Bordering the plateau in the south are the Himalayas, including Mount Everest called Jumulangma Feng by the Chinese, on the China-Nepal border.

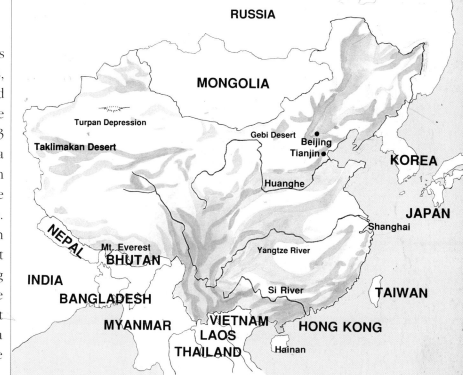

RUSSIA

MONGOLIA

Turpan Depression

Taklimakan Desert

Gebi Desert
Beijing
Tianjin

KOREA

Huanghe

JAPAN

Shanghai

NEPAL

Mt. Everest
BHUTAN

Yangtze River

INDIA

TAIWAN

BANGLADESH

Si River

HONG KONG

MYANMAR

VIETNAM
LAOS
THAILAND

Hainan

The uniquely shaped hills of Guilin in southwestern China are a favorite subject of Chinese painters.

DESERTS AND PLAINS

Elevations drop to between 6,560 and 3,280 feet (1,999 and 1,000 m) toward the famous grasslands of Mongolia, and the Gobi Desert.

In the northwest is the Taklimakan Desert, the largest in China, through which the ancient Silk Road once passed. North of the desert is the Tian Shan range. The Turpan Depression, an oasis at the northern edge of the Taklimakan Desert, is the lowest point in China at 505 feet (154 m) below sea level, where temperatures can reach 120°F (48.9°C).

In the southern provinces, the terrain changes to unusually shaped cliffs, gorges, and waterfalls.

Toward the coast in the east, elevations drop to around 1,500 feet (457 m). This area is the great plains region of China and the focus of agriculture and human settlement.

China's major rivers help to shape the coastline as they carry silt toward the sea. One billion tons of silt carried by the Yellow River extend its delta by 9 square miles (25 square km) annually.

CLIMATE

Most of China has a temperate climate, but with striking extremes—harsh northern Siberian frosts, arid western deserts, and lush tropical weather in the southeast. Although China spans four time zones, the whole country follows the same time as its capital, Beijing.

Northern winters are bitter cold, with temperatures dropping to -18°F (-27.8°C). In the northern city of Harbin it is cold enough for a winter-long exhibition of ice sculptures.

Provinces in the north and northwest may experience extreme weather conditions within a single day—freezing cold in the morning, hot by midday. Springtime in the north brings sandstorms from Mongolia, blowing fine sand everywhere, even through the tiniest cracks in buildings.

Winter in Beijing, the capital of China. Winter days in northern China are sunny, dry—and cold.

China is officially divided into north and south by the Yangtze River. As the south is warmer than the north, people in cities south of the river do not have central heating in their buildings. In winter, it is not surprising to find residents of cities just south of the river bundled up to keep warm. In the Yangtze River delta near the coast, the weather is warm and humid with four distinct seasons. Here, winters are much shorter, with the average temperature around 32°F (0°C).

Summers in the north can be as punishing as winters. Temperatures can reach highs of 100°F (37.8°C) or more. Autumn is cool and dry.

The Yangtze River is China's main waterway, linking the interior with seaports and major cities. Large ships can travel as far as Wuhan, 700 miles (1,127 km) upriver from the coast. However, only 1,700 miles (2,736 km), or less than half, of the river are navigable.

WATERWAYS

YANGTZE RIVER Also known as Changjiang, or Long River, the Yangtze rises in the Qinghai-Tibetan mountains. Measuring 3,915 miles (6,301 km), it is the longest river in China and the third longest in the world. It flows through nine provinces, emptying into the East China Sea near Shanghai.

The Yangtze officially divides China into north and south. It has 700 tributaries and flows through important industrial and agricultural areas. Half of China's crops are grown in the Yangtze delta, especially rice, the country's staple food.

HUANG HE The Huang He, or Yellow River, starts as melting snow in the Qinghai-Tibetan mountains. Its 3,395-mile (5,464-km) journey traverses nine provinces before it empties into the Bohai Sea. As it flows through the central Loess Plateau, it picks up an incredible amount of loose yellow soil, which gives the river its name.

The Huang He has been called "China's Sorrow," for it has flooded its

THE GRAND CANAL

The Grand Canal (*right*) is the oldest and longest manmade canal in China. The earliest parts were dug in the fifth century B.C. This 1,105-mile (1,778-km) canal was an immense project in terms of labor and lives lost.

During the Sui Dynasty (A.D. 581–618) the then capital of Luoyang was linked to the old capital of Xi'an. The canal was gradually extended over the centuries by various emperors to join Hangzhou in the south and Beijing in the north. Construction was finally completed at the end of the 13th century. The main function of the canal was to move troops in times of war, but it was also used to transport food from the fertile south to the barren north. This gradually made the south the agricultural center of China.

The Grand Canal connects four major rivers—the Huang He, Yangtze, Huai, and Qiantang. It passes through some of the prettiest parts of China.

Much of the canal has fallen into disuse due to the construction of road and railway links and the flooding of the Huang He. Now, only one-third of the original canal is in use, mainly to transport agricultural products and raw materials to factories and warehouses. It is also used to irrigate the drought-prone areas of Hubei, Henan, and Anhui provinces.

banks more than a thousand times, destroying crops and killing countless people. One billion tons of silt carried downstream each year, make the Huang He the muddiest river in the world. The riverbed rises by 4 inches (10 cm) annually, overflowing its banks. The silt buildup has, over the centuries, caused the river to change course 12 times. Near its estuary, the water is so thick and low that there is little marine life.

The Huang He is also known as the cradle of Chinese civilization, for it was along the fertile banks of this river that land in China was first cultivated. From these beginnings, villages, towns, and empires grew.

XI RIVER Also known as the Zhujiang, this 1,216-mile (1,957-km) river traverses the southern provinces before it flows into the South China Sea.

Beijingers on their bicycles, the main mode of transportation in Chinese cities.

CITIES

BEIJING Beijing is China's capital. With a history of more than 800 years, it is China's political, economic, scientific, and cultural center and contains some of the country's finest buildings and palaces.

In the center of Beijing is Tiananmen Square. The largest public square in the world, it can hold up to one million people. On the northern side is the Tiananmen Gate, the Gate of Heavenly Peace, which was once used as the main gate to the Ming and Qing imperial palaces; today visitors still use this gate as the entrance to the Forbidden City. From the gate, on October 1, 1949, Mao Zedong proclaimed the founding of the People's Republic of China. During the Qing Dynasty, the square was enclosed by a red wall and commoners only entered it to be executed.

With a population of about 14 million people, this bustling commercial city with its numerous foreign embassies is also the seat of government. China's 23 provinces, five autonomous regions, four municipalities, and two special administrative regions are administered from Beijing.

FORBIDDEN CITY

This famous complex of buildings (*right*) in Beijing is so called because once, only the emperor and his court could live there. This cluster of imperial palaces was originally built in A.D. 1406–20 during the Ming Dynasty. It is surrounded by a wide moat and a high wall. There are 9,999 rooms. If a newborn prince lived in a different room every day of his life, he would be 27 years old by the time he had seen them all!

The area around the Forbidden City is equally interesting. Medieval buildings are still standing that once held businesses catering to the needs of the people in nearby palaces. In fact, the imperial pharmacy is still in business and dispenses the same kind of pills and potions that used to cure princes; the royal shoe shop is not far off.

SHANGHAI Shanghai sits at the meeting point of two rivers: the Huangpu and Wusong. The city has always been an important port in China and today handles the country's largest amount of freight annually.

In the mid-19th century, after the Opium Wars, Shanghai opened its doors to the West. Foreign banks, shops, and embassies were built, all with a distinct European flavor. The Shanghainese were exposed to a more Western lifestyle and thought themselves more sophisticated than their fellow Chinese elsewhere. Shanghai was once called the "Paris of the East" and the style of that era can be seen in the old buildings.

Shanghai is one of China's most densely populated cities, with about 17 million inhabitants. In the city center, there are about 19,000 people per square mile (7,336 per square km).

Numerous foreign entrepreneurs and technicians have settled in Shanghai, strengthening its claim to be China's most international metropolis.

The busy streets of Guangzhou. In the early 19th century, the city was a center of anti-imperial activity and revolutionary movements.

GUANGZHOU Guangzhou (formerly Canton) is the capital of Guangdong province. Guangzhou is one of the most ancient Chinese cities, with a history that goes back 20 centuries. Legend says that five gods came riding into the city on five rams. Each brought a six-eared rice plant so that the town would forever be free of famine. The gods vanished, and the rams turned into stone. Today there is a sculpture of five rams in the city, which is still known as the "City of Rams."

Guangzhou sits on the fertile Pearl River delta, facing the South China Sea. Because of its position, it was visited by Indian and Roman merchants as far back as the second century A.D. It is now an important trading and industrial city.

Cantonese, the local dialect, is commonly spoken in the city. Being in the far south of China, Guangzhou is warm and moist almost all year. It has lush green vegetation, abundant rice fields, and fruit orchards.

Over 10 million people live in this vibrant city, which is one of the most modern and enterprising places in China.

FLORA AND FAUNA

China's plant life includes nearly all species of plants found in both the frigid and temperate zones. Plants that existed in the Ice Age have been found growing in some hidden corners of the country. Forests are filled with cypress, pine, and bamboo. There are also hundreds of varieties of chrysanthemum and peony.

China's range of wildlife is equally impressive. There are over 100 species of rare endangered animals, including the giant panda, golden monkey, Manchurian tiger, and snow leopard. More than 600 nature reserves have been formed to protect China's flora and fauna.

THE GIANT PANDA

The giant panda (*right*), China's favorite animal, is threatened with extinction. Pandas live on a diet only of bamboo leaves. With urbanization, more bamboo plants are being destroyed, forcing the pandas to go higher up into the mountains in search of food. Bamboo has a very slow growth cycle. Some species can take up to 100 years to grow to maturity. Unfortunately, many pandas die of starvation due to the shrinking bamboo forests. Early 1990s data indicated that about 1,000 pandas are living in their natural habitat in parts of Sichuan, Shaanxi, and Gansu provinces.

HISTORY

MORE THAN HALF A MILLION YEARS AGO, primitive human beings lived in China. Evidence of *homo erectus*, estimated to be around 420,000 years old, were first found near Beijing in the 1920s. These fossils included partial skeletal remains, stone tools, and animal bones. In 1929, the first complete skull was discovered, the remains of the Peking Man.

THE FIRST DYNASTY

Accounts of the legendary period before the 22nd century B.C. mingle fact and fiction—rulers were immortal and dragons and other mythical creatures such as phoenixes and griffons prowled the earth. At this time there arose the Xia Dynasty (2205–1766 B.C.). Archeological evidence indicates that the Xia were descended from a widespread Yellow River valley Neolithic culture called Longshan, famous for its black-lacquered pottery. The Xia were overthrown by the Shang (1766–1123 B.C.).

Opposite: **The Great Wall of China, the only man-made structure visible from the Moon.**

CHINA'S CIVILIZATIONS

Legendary Period	pre-23rd century B.C.	Sui Dynasty	581–618
Xia Dynasty	2205–1766 B.C.	Tang Dynasty	618–907
Shang Dynasty	1766–1123 B.C.	Five Dynasties	907–960
Western Zhou Dynasty	1122–770 B.C.	Northern Song Dynasty	960–1127
Eastern Zhou Dynasty		Southern Song Dynasty	1127–1279
Spring and Autumn Period	770–476 B.C.	Liao Dynasty	906–1125
Warring States Period	475–221 B.C.	Western Xia Dynasty	1038–1227
Qin Dynasty	221–206 B.C.	Jin Dynasty	1115–1234
Western Han Dynasty	206 B.C.–A.D. 24	Yuan Dynasty (Mongolian)	1271–1368
Eastern Han Dynasty	25–220	Ming Dynasty	1368–1644
The Three Kingdoms	220–280	Qing Dynasty (Manchurian)	1644–1911
Western Jin Dynasty	265–316	Republic of China	1912–1949
Eastern Jin Dynasty	317–420	People's Republic of China	1949 to present
Northern and Southern dynasties	420–581		

A wall mural depicting a scene from the Spring and Autumn period, a time of disorder and chaos as feudal states fought one another for power.

SHANG AND ZHOU DYNASTIES

Records of daily life in urban societies during the Shang Dynasty have been found carved on bones, tortoise shells, and bronze.

The Shang were conquered by the Zhou, who ruled by a feudal system in which leaders of the different states of the empire swore loyalty and paid taxes to the emperor.

The discovery of iron casting during this period resulted in improved farm tools, and the development of large scale irrigation. The resulting prosperity made China one of the most advanced civilizations in the world at that time. Also during this time Taoism and Confucianism evolved, introducing ideas that are still evident in Chinese thinking today.

After 200 years of peace, the Zhou Dynasty disintegrated into smaller squabbling states (Spring and Autumn period) that later grouped into larger states (Warring States period).

QIN SHIHUANG

China was truly united for the first time under Qin Shihuang (221–206 B.C.), or "the first exalted emperor." He ascended the throne of the state of Qin at the age of 13 and went on to conquer the surrounding states. He completed his conquest of the other states in 221 B.C. As the first emperor, he is remembered for both the great and the terrible things he did.

Qin Shihuang abolished the feudal system and established a new order of society that was to last for 2,000 years. People were divided into different classes: aristocrats, landowners, bureaucrats, peasants, merchants, and slaves.

The emperor set up a central government and an imperial examination was started to recruit the best scholars as civil servants. This stressed the importance of learning, raised the level of education and culture, and made China a nation ruled by scholars.

Qin Shihuang also standardized the written language, the system of weights and measures, and a form of currency. Transportation links to the capital, such as roads and canals, were built.

A shrewd and jealous man, Qin Shihuang was well-known for his tyranny. It is said that he buried alive hundreds of scholars whose views were different from his or who appeared to be smarter than he was. He also burned thousands of books for the same reason. Precious works of great philosophers such as Confucius and Mencius were destroyed; what we read now was rewritten from memory by scholars.

In 1974, farmers digging a well in Xi'an discovered a vault containing 6,000 life-sized terracotta warriors depicted in full uniform and arranged in battle formation protecting Qin Shihuang's nearby tomb.

Upon becoming king of Qin, one of Qin Shihuang's first acts was to start construction of his tomb, 19 miles (30 km) east of Xi'an. A first-century chronicle records that 700,000 workmen spent 36 years completing a mini-universe of a mausoleum, featuring rivers of mercury, jewels embedded in the ceiling to represent stars, and crossbows to deter intruders.

THE GREAT WALL

The Great Wall (*above*), symbol of China's ancient civilization, stretches for 4,160 miles (6,695 km) across northern China. This colossal monument is the only manmade structure that can be seen with the naked eye from the moon. Its construction started during the Spring and Autumn period (770–476 B.C.). Rival feudal kingdoms built walls around their territories to keep out invading nomadic tribes from the north. When Qin Shihuang unified China, he began to link up and extend these walls.

Prisoners of war, convicts, soldiers, civilians, and farmers labored to build the Great Wall. Millions died of starvation, disease, and exhaustion during the construction. Their bodies were buried in the foundations or used as part of the wall. Any materials found nearby—clay, stone, willow branches, reeds, and sand—were used.

The Great Wall crosses loess plateaus, mountains, deserts, rivers, and valleys, passing through five provinces and two autonomous regions. It is about 20 feet (6 m) wide and 26 feet (8 m) high. Parts of the wall are so broad that 10 soldiers can walk abreast.

Parts of the old wall can still be seen in remote parts of China. Most visitors see the portions that were restored during the Ming Dynasty, when stone slabs replaced clay bricks. The wall took 100 years to rebuild, and it is said that the amount of material used in the present wall alone is enough to circle the world at the equator five times.

HAN DYNASTY

The Han Dynasty (206 B.C.–A.D. 220) was one of the most important dynasties to rule China. Established after the overthrow of Qin Shihuang, the Han Dynasty was of such significance that even today the Chinese refer to themselves as "men of Han."

The Han Dynasty ruled over a vast area: from the Pamir Mountains in today's Afghanistan in the west to Korea in the east, and from Mongolia in the north to Vietnam in the south.

There were many notable achievements during Han rule. Trade flourished and China was opened to other cultures. The legendary Silk Road was well-traveled and contacts were made with Central and West Asia and even with Rome.

Buddhism was introduced from India, and Confucianism became the state doctrine. A thorough knowledge of Confucian classics became essential for officials and candidates for the civil service. Painting and the arts also flourished and many historical and philosophical works were written.

In addition, a new style of writing well-suited for the compilation of official documents was developed. The first Chinese dictionary was compiled in A.D. 100. Containing 9,000 words, it explained the meanings of the words and provided examples of the different forms of the words used in writing.

Advancements were made in science and technology. Water clocks and sundials were used by officials. Paper was invented and a seismograph developed.

The Han Dynasty lasted 400 years. Eventually a succession of corrupt and weak rulers led to its downfall.

The Han Dynasty was founded by Liu Bang, a rebel peasant who once urinated into the hat of a court scholar to show his disdain for education. Nevertheless he later proved himself a practical and flexible ruler, and had learned men in his court.

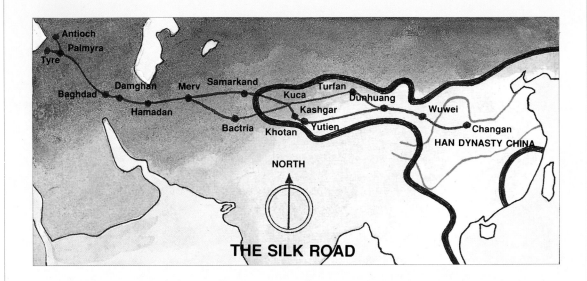

THE SILK ROAD

THE SILK ROAD

The ancient Silk Road was established some 2,000 years ago. Starting at Changan, the ancient capital (present-day Xi'an), it stretched westward for 4,350 miles (7,000 km) crossing mountains and deserts all the way to the eastern coast of the Mediterranean. From there, trade goods were taken to Constantinople (Istanbul in present-day Turkey), Rome, and Venice.

Chinese silk and other Chinese inventions, such as paper, printing from wood blocks, gunpowder, and the compass, made their way to East Asia, the Middle East, and Europe along this route. In turn, merchants introduced foreign religions, art, and cultures to China. They also brought agricultural products and the Chinese soon began eating grapes, walnuts, cucumbers, broad beans, and watermelon. Silk was also exchanged for Persian horses, glass, perfume, and ivory.

Merchants traveled the Silk Road on camels. Chosen because of their docile temper and their endurance of the sun and sand, these animals carried enormous loads across mountains and deserts. But few people traveled the entire span of the road; goods were passed from one middleman to another along the route.

Later, with the loss of Roman territory in Asia, the Silk Road became overrun by bandits and few people traveled it. In the 13th and 14th centuries, the Mongol rulers of China revived the use of the road by which Marco Polo, the Italian merchant-adventurer, arrived in Mongol-ruled China.

DYNASTIC TRANSITION

For the next 400 years China was divided into separate kingdoms constantly fighting for power. The nomadic tribes from the north succeeded for a while in gaining a foothold in China. Four dynasties followed the Han Dynasty—the Western Jin, Eastern Jin, Northern and Southern dynasties, and the Sui. The Sui Dynasty went bankrupt because of large expansion programs in public works and expeditions to Central Asia. Nevertheless, the Sui Dynasty laid the groundwork for the greatest Chinese dynasty, the Tang.

A wall mural showing Tang court maidens.

TANG DYNASTY

The Tang Dynasty lasted 300 years from A.D. 618 to 907, during which time Central Asia, Korea, and northern Vietnam came under China's rule. The Tang period is considered the Golden Age of China. Improvements to agriculture and farming tools increased food production. Government administration was in the hands of top Confucian scholars. Chinese arts and literature flourished and the art of printing was developed.

Although Tang rule gradually deteriorated and was overthrown by the Songs, no other dynasty matched the Tang impact on China. Many dynasties that followed were modeled on the Tang Dynasty in the hope of reaching the same heights of glory. None did.

THE FOUR GREAT INVENTIONS OF ANCIENT CHINA

Many things that we take for granted in everyday life were invented in China. For example, the umbrella, eyeglasses, paper money, kites, the mechanical clock, and even the washboard made their way to the West after being developed in China. The most important four inventions from ancient China are paper, printing, gunpowder, and the compass.

PAPER Before paper was invented, the Chinese carved characters on bone and tortoiseshell. Later, the first book was bound using strips of bamboo held together with string. People then started writing on silk, which proved too expensive.

Paper first made its appearance in the Han Dynasty. Bark, bits of hemp, cloth, and old fishing nets were boiled to a pulp. This was rinsed, pounded flat, and spread out on fine bamboo screens to form sheets of paper.

PRINTING At first, printing blocks contained only one page of text, so each block could only be used to produce the same page of a book. During the Song Dynasty, single characters were engraved on individual blocks of wood. Each character could then be used over and over. Assembled into pages, they were inked and moistened paper was placed over them.

GUNPOWDER During the period of the Warring States, alchemists trying to make immortality pills discovered that a mixture of sulphur and saltpeter caused an explosion when heated.

At first, the new discovery was used for firecrackers. Later, gunpowder was used in war, for the first time during the Tang Dynasty.

COMPASS The compass was first used more than 2,000 years ago when the Chinese discovered that a piece of natural magnetite would automatically point in a north-south direction. The Chinese soon started to fashion magnets of ingenious design. One was of a wooden figure on a horse-drawn chariot, and no matter which direction the chariot turned, the figure would always be pointing north.

Compasses became common as navigational devices on ships between 850 and 1050.

THE LAST DYNASTY

China came under imperial rule for the last time in 1644 when the Ming Dynasty was overthrown by Manchurians from the north.

The Qing Dynasty (1644–1911) lasted over 200 years, ruling over territory that included Manchuria, Mongolia, Tibet, Taiwan, and Turkestan (Xinjiang). The empire had never been larger. For the first 150 years, the country was well-run and prospered under able emperors. Success gave way to power struggles among corrupt court officials.

Few Europeans traveled in China as only the port of Canton (Guangzhou) was open to them. They came to buy Chinese goods such as tea, silk, and porcelain, but they could not sell anything as China was largely self-sufficient. In order to balance the trade, the British started selling opium to the Chinese in the 1780s. The Qing government tried to ban its sale, but corrupt officials and merchants did nothing to stop it. This soon led to a series of wars known as the Opium Wars, in which the Chinese were defeated by the British and their society devastated.

In submitting to British demands in the Treaty of Nanking (1842), the Qing government granted land to the British and allowed them to open several more ports to trade. Hong Kong became a British colony. Other European nations also forced the government to sign similar treaties.

China was soon in debt and its people heavily taxed. Soon, the Taiping Rebellion broke out in the south. This weakened the Manchurians even more, as Britain, France, and Russia took the opportunity to occupy even more Chinese land. The Qing Dynasty finally collapsed in 1911.

The Summer Palace built by Empress Cixi of the Qing Dynasty in 1873. She took money meant for the modernization of the navy to build the palace. Misuse of funds and aggression from outsiders led to the weakening and eventual collapse of the Qing Dynasty.

Above: **A statue of Sun Yat-sen in Jiangsu province. Sun is known as the father of modern China.**

Opposite: **A portrait of Mao Zedong in Tiananmen Square.**

MODERN CHINA

Sun Yat-sen, leader of the Kuomintang (Nationalist Party), established the Republic of China in 1911 and became its president. However, the new republic was not at peace as partisans in various parts of the country fought for power. One in particular, Yuan Shi Kai, a former Qing minister, controlled much of northern China. In order to keep the peace, Sun gave up the presidency to Yuan.

Yuan declared himself emperor in 1912 and made Beijing his capital. He died after being in power for three weeks and China was back in the hands of partisans. From the south, Sun Yat-sen tried to fight the partisans and arouse national concern, but he was unsuccessful.

In 1919, at the Versailles Peace Conference that ended World War I, the German concessions in Shandong were handed over to Japan instead of being returned to the Chinese. This sparked off the May Fourth Movement. Workers and intellectuals boycotted Japanese goods and demonstrated against foreign intervention and all things connected with feudal China.

What started out as a protest at Beijing University spread to every part of the country and became a national movement toward modernization.

NATIONALISTS AND COMMUNISTS When Sun Yat-sen died in 1925, his colleague, Chiang Kai-shek, took over. Chiang succeeded in unifying China by defeating the partisans in the north. He made Nanjing his capital.

Chiang then began to fight the Communists who had formed a political party in 1921. The Kuomintang drove the Communists into the southern mountains, from where Mao Zedong—who in 1911 had joined Sun Yat-sen's revolutionary army to overthrow the Qing Dynasty and had also served in the Kuomintang under Sun's leadership—led an army, using guerilla warfare against the nationalist forces.

In 1934, led by Mao, the Communists began a heroic journey known as the Long March. Traveling a distance of 7,000 miles (11,200 km) on foot over some of the harshest parts of the country, they arrived in Shaanxi in the northwest and set up their headquarters there in 1935.

Chiang Kai-shek, determined to eliminate the Communists, overlooked the danger presented by Japanese troops moving into China. Even when the Sino-Japanese War began in 1937, Chiang went on fighting the Communists.

One of Chiang's own generals finally arrested him and forced him to make an alliance with the Communists to fight the Japanese, who had occupied eastern China. By the end of World War II in 1945, the Japanese, defeated by the Americans in the Pacific, moved out of China.

Then civil war broke out between the Kuomintang and the Communist Party, as both sides fought to gain control of China. The Communist People's Liberation Army, which had the support of the peasants, defeated the nationalists in 1949. In 1950 the Kuomintang fled to Taiwan and they have since ruled the island as the Republic of China.

THE PEOPLE'S REPUBLIC OF CHINA

On October 1, 1949, Mao Zedong declared the founding of the People's Republic of China. China was in economic trouble after so many years of fighting wars. The Communist Party had not only to establish a new political system, but also to revive the economy and put it on par with other countries. By 1953 the economy had recovered considerably. Encouraged by this success, Mao Zedong launched a campaign in 1958 known as the Great Leap Forward.

A painting depicting the declaration of the founding of the People's Republic of China by Mao Zedong on October 1, 1949.

THE GREAT LEAP FORWARD   The countryside was divided into communes with 5,000 households each so that labor was used effectively. Everyone ate in a communal hall, children were looked after in boarding schools, and people worked in fields and factories. Crop yields increased, and industrial output such as steel production went up by as much as 50 percent.

Spurred by this success, the government took more peasants out of the fields to work in factories. However, agriculture began to suffer and the peasants were exhausted. Then floods and droughts drove the country into famine. The campaign was aborted in 1960, and Mao was forced to take a backseat as some party members, including Deng Xiaoping, began to get the economy into shape again.

THE CULTURAL REVOLUTION In 1966 Mao tried to regain control by starting the Cultural Revolution. Claiming that China was threatened by capitalism, he called for a rebellion against the "four olds"—old ideas, old culture, old habits, and old customs. China was caught up in a frenzy of destruction. Books were burned, relics destroyed, and temples torn down.

Homes of intellectuals and people suspected of harboring the four olds were smashed, and they and their families were thrown into prison or sent to the countryside to work. Among these was Deng Xiaoping.

China's recovery from this calamity was ably accomplished by the respected premier Zhou Enlai who worked to repair the damage to the economy. Both Zhou Enlai and Mao Zedong died in 1976, and the Cultural Revolution ended. Deng Xiaoping won the ensuing power struggle.

China under Deng Xiaoping underwent radical reform. Economic packages introduced in 1979 helped the country prosper and China opened its doors to foreign travelers and businesses. Nevertheless, political problems persisted. In June 1989 clashes in Tiananmen Square between students demonstrating for democracy and the People's Liberation Army resulted in great loss of life.

A demonstration in support of the Cultural Revolution, which gave rise to a group of young people called the Red Guards, who went on a rampage of destruction.

AFTER TIANANMEN After Tiananmen, foreign investments flowing into China were cut back drastically and nations meted out economic sanctions on the country. Deng Xiaoping had paid a heavy price. However, life went on and Deng planned for the future. He paved the way for a new generation of leaders after him, led by Jiang Zemin. In 1992, Deng's official visit to the south once again fueled a new round of economic development and the inflow of foreign capital.

Deng died in 1997 and his successors have worked to ensure economic growth and social stability in the past few years. In 2001, China entered the World Trade Organization and yet another generation of leaders is expected to take the helm.

GOVERNMENT

CHINA HAS BEEN RULED by the Chinese Communist Party (CCP) since 1949. Founded in 1921, its policies and beliefs are based on the ideas of Marxism-Leninism combined with "Mao Thought," which hinges on the notion that the highest phase of human society should be a Communist one, where properties are owned by all and there are no classes.

China's constitution provides for the CCP's operation alongside other parties, but there are no truly independent parties. National political activity is managed by the CCP through its members in high-level government offices. Political activities differing from the CCP's objectives are restricted, hampering the rise of any significant opposition. The system of government is essentially one-party rule.

Above: **The National Emblem of the People's Republic of China.**

Opposite: **The entrance to a government office complex in Nanjing. The lintel is inscribed with the writing of Sun Yatsen. The words mean "All efforts are for the common good."**

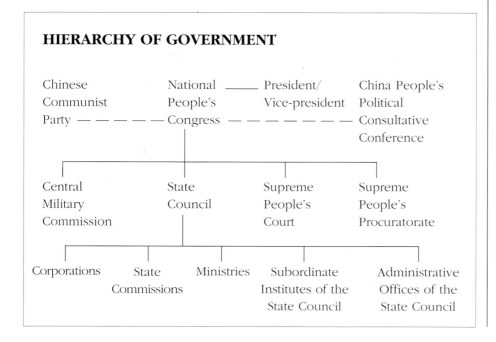

HIERARCHY OF GOVERNMENT

Chinese Communist Party — — — — — National People's Congress — — — — — — — President/Vice-president — China People's Political Consultative Conference

Central Military Commission

State Council

Supreme People's Court

Supreme People's Procuratorate

Corporations

State Commissions

Ministries

Subordinate Institutes of the State Council

Administrative Offices of the State Council

Soldiers in the Forbidden City. The Chinese army, known as the People's Liberation Army, is administered by the Central Military Commission.

GOVERNMENT HIERARCHY

THE PRESIDENT AND VICE-PRESIDENT The president is the official head of state. The vice-president takes his place when the president is unable to perform formal duties. The president's office is mainly ceremonial and power lies with the Communist Party's general secretary, a post which the current president holds.

THE NATIONAL PEOPLE'S CONGRESS (NPC) The National People's Congress is the highest organ of state power in China, with the power to amend the constitution and make laws. It also elects the president, vice-president, chairman of the Central Military Commission, president of the Supreme People's Court, and procurator-general and approves the nomination of the premier (prime minister) by the president and the members of the State Council. The NPC is made up of deputies elected from the provinces, autonomous regions, and municipalities. It meets once a year in Beijing to decide on major issues affecting the country.

THE STATE COUNCIL The State Council enforces the laws and decisions of the NPC and has the power to adopt administrative measures and issue orders. It is made up of the premier, vice-premiers, state councilors, ministers, the auditor-general, and the secretary-general. The premier has overall responsibility and directs the work of the State Council.

THE CENTRAL MILITARY COMMISSION Headed by a chairman, the Central Military Commission commands the People's Liberation Army (PLA), the People's Armed Police Force, and the militia. It is accountable to the NPC.

THE SUPREME PEOPLE'S COURT AND PEOPLE'S PROCURATORATE The people's courts and procuratorates try criminal and civil cases and uphold China's legal system.

MINISTRIES AND STATE COMMISSIONS Ministries and state commissions are part of the State Council. They issue orders and regulations in accordance with the law and decisions of the State Council. Some administrations and bureaus with special areas of work—such as the Economic Legislation Research Center, Nuclear Power Administration, Foreign Exports Bureau, and State Administration for Taxation—report directly to the State Council instead of to their respective ministries.

CHINESE PEOPLE'S POLITICAL CONSULTATIVE CONFERENCE (CPPCC) The CPPCC is an advisory body that holds consultations and offers opinions on important issues in China's political system. It consists of representatives from the Communist Party, public figures, and people's organizations.

Since 1949, China has had four constitutions—in 1954, 1975, 1978, and 1982. These resulted from changing circumstances. The 1982 Constitution guaranteed freedom of speech and religious beliefs, the right to vote and run for election, and the right to employment and education. It also helped to speed up the economic reform program known as the Four Modernizations. In 1999 the constitution formally recognized the role of private entrepreneurs in China's economy. By 2000, China had 1.76 million private firms employing 20.11 million people or half the urban work force.

Homeward bound on a donkey cart. At the lowest level, the administrative unit is the residents' committee.

ADMINISTRATIVE DIVISIONS

China is divided into 23 provinces, five autonomous regions, four municipalities, and two special administrative regions (SAR).

Each province is divided into cities, counties, and towns. Administrative units at the lowest level are the Residents' Committees. They manage public welfare, settle disputes, see to public security, and ensure that state rules are implemented and observed. They also adopt, issue, and decide on plans for the economic and social welfare of their districts.

China's five autonomous regions are Inner Mongolia, Ningxia, Xinjiang, Guangxi, and Tibet (Xizang). These areas have large communities of minority nationalities. Local people's congresses and governments are set up to exercise the right of limited self-government.

The four municipalities—Beijing, Shanghai, Tianjin, and Chongqing—report directly to the central government.

ADMINISTRATIVE DIVISIONS

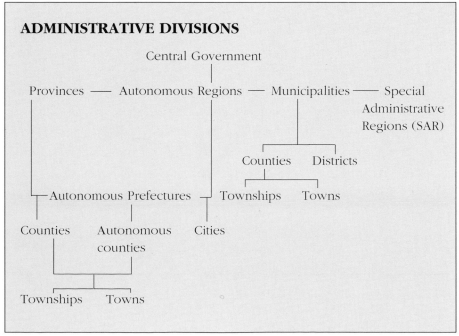

The Great Hall of the People on Tiananmen Square, Beijing, was built in 1959 and completed in less than a year. The National People's Congress meets here. Formal meetings and receptions for visiting heads of state and government also take place in the Great Hall.

ECONOMY

AFTER THE COMMUNIST PARTY took power in 1949, the economy was collectivized. The government seized private enterprises with agriculture, industry, and commerce under collective ownership. Everyone was to contribute to and benefit from common goals.

However, under this system, agricultural and industrial production stagnated, and economic growth slowed. In the 1980s China began reforms aimed at making it a market-socialist economy. For the first time in years, the Chinese could own small businesses. Farmers were allowed and encouraged to grow produce for their own profit and to sell it in the "free market."

Above: **A free market in Lijiang, where farmers take their excess produce to sell after meeting the government quota.**

Opposite: **Shanghai's famous waterfront, The Bund, flanked by modern skyscrapers. More cars are apparent on the streets with rising affluence.**

To encourage workers, a bonus system was introduced. Besides their basic wage, workers got bonuses for productivity, punctuality, perfect attendance, and for having a good work attitude. Trade links with other countries were encouraged and special economic zones allowed foreign investors to build factories and operate businesses.

Since China began to liberalize the economy in 1980, there has been enormous economic progress. In the 1990s China's annual gross domestic product (GDP) grew by 152 percent to $1 trillion in 2001. This is more than seven times that of the GDP in 1978. Current forecasts for up to 2005 indicate an annual growth rate of 7 percent.

Rice terraces in south-western China.

AGRICULTURE

Although China is mainly an agricultural country, only about 13.5 percent of its vast expanse of land is suitable for cultivation. Even so, China is one of the largest producers of food in the world, feeding 1.3 billion people at home and exporting rice to several countries including Japan, Korea, the Philippines, Indonesia, Iraq, Russia, and Cote d'Ivoire.

As a result of reforms in the agricultural system, farmers had incentive to produce more, and agricultural production tripled between 1978 and 1991. China is now one of the world's leading producers of grain, cotton, and rapeseed.

In the north, where the weather is cold and dry, wheat, millet, and sorghum are grown. Wheat is made into bread and noodles, while sorghum is used as a food substitute or as fodder and may be made into wine.

THE BACKBONE OF THE ECONOMY

Farmers (*right*) make up 63.9 percent of the population of China and are the backbone of the country's economy. After the Communists took power in 1949, China's agricultural system was reorganized. Cooperatives, and later communes, were formed in which farmers pooled their land and resources and shared their collective income.

In 1979 there was another reorganization: farming households were allowed to work on a piece of land and, in return, had to deliver to the government an agreed amount of produce. They were allowed to keep any extra produce. This yielded good results, and by the mid-80s many farm families were growing extra produce or raising animals for their own profit.

Chinese farmers use simple agricultural tools. Few can afford tractors or combine harvestors. In the past they had to gather human and animal manure as fertilizer. This is seldom done now as chemical fertilizers are cheap and easily available.

During the nonfarming months, farmers find temporary employment in cottage industries or turn to trade, like selling cooked food or bamboo ware.

Rice is the most important crop in the south. It is grown mainly in the Yangtze River valley and on the Yunnan-Guizhou plateau. About half of the cultivated land in China is used for growing rice, and crops are harvested twice a year.

Corn and soybeans are major crops in both the north and south. Protein-rich soybeans are an important part of the Chinese diet. Nonfood crops include cotton, rapeseed, and tobacco.

On the flat grasslands of Mongolia, sheep and goats are raised. China now produces enough lamb for its own consumption and for export. Dairy products come from cows raised on the outskirts of large cities.

Above: **A metalwork plant in Wuhan. Steel and iron smelting are top money-earning industries.**

Opposite: **Shanghai's port handles the largest amount of freight in China annually.**

INDUSTRY

China manufactures heavy industrial goods such as cars, trucks, planes, trains, and ships and finished products such as electrical appliances and other consumer goods. China's most important industries include oil, iron and steel, coal, energy, machinery, electronics, and textiles.

The industrial sector grew slowly after the 1979 economic reforms due to the emphasis on agriculture and light industry. This changed in the 1990s. With increasing emphasis on industry, by 2000 industrial production had grown by 9.9 percent, due mainly to foreign investment. There are now many foreign company enterprises in textiles and garments, electronics, chemicals, energy, transportation, and construction. Since 1979, China has approved an estimated 360,000 foreign-funded enterprises, with an investment value of $348 billion.

While most industries are scattered along the coast, industrial areas are being developed throughout the country. Guangdong province in the south has the strongest industrial growth as investors from neighboring Hong Kong have set up factories and businesses.

A significant development in China was the establishment of two stock exchanges in Shanghai and Shenzhen in 1991. Both local Chinese and foreigners are allowed to trade stocks.

SPECIAL ECONOMIC ZONES

China has established five Special Economic Zones (SEZs) in Shenzhen, Zhuhai, Shantou in Guangdong, Xiamen in Fujian, and Hainan, the largest. These were set up because China realized that in order to catch up with the rest of the world, it not only needed foreign money, but also foreign technology and expertise. The SEZs offer incentives to foreign investors with capital and technology. The zones have boosted the country's overall economic growth.

Between 1980 and 2000 these zones have played a critical role in revitalizing industry. For instance, in 20 years, Shenzhen's GDP grew by 30 percent annually. But the contribution to the national GDP by the five zones has gradually shrunk as other parts of the country have caught up in economic development. The total contribution by the zones now amounts to 3 percent of China's exports and accounts for about 15 percent of the total foreign investment.

Shenzhen, the first economic zone to be developed, is just next to Hong Kong. Investors are attracted by Shenzhen's low taxes, low operating costs, and cheap, abundant labor. Shenzhen also has land and raw materials, and its proximity to Hong Kong brings it closer to world markets.

ENVIRONMENT

CHINA'S RAPID ECONOMIC GROWTH in the past 20 years has been accompanied by severe deterioration of the environment. Air and water pollution levels are among the highest in the world, and this has led to premature deaths from pollution-related respiratory illnesses.

Many waterways in the country are contaminated by industrial waste, making them unfit for human use. The cost of reversing ecological destruction and cleaning up environmental pollution is estimated to be $150 billion— 14 percent of the gross domestic product.

Nevertheless efforts made by the Chinese government since 1990 have slowed down deterioration of the environment. The government has made environmental protection a high priority. It has implemented programs and projects at the national and local level and effected economic reform policies on industry with stricter regulations in polluted areas.

Conservation efforts include reforestation, river basin management, energy and nature conservation, the switch to natural gas use, controlling industrial water and air pollution as well as vehicle emissions particularly in urban areas, and recycling.

In addition, there has been much growth in the domestic environmental protection industry in recent years. By the end of 2000, there were more than 10,000 institutions and enterprises. Set to grow at 15 percent annually, the industry output value will be $24 billion by the end of 2005.

Above: **2000 Climate Conference, Netherlands. China, as the world's second biggest emitter of carbon dioxide, is part of global efforts to reduce greenhouse gases.**

Opposite: **Boat travel along a scenic tree-lined river.**

Chinese cheer on July 13, 2001 in downtown Beijing moments after the announcement that China had won the bid to host the Olympics Games in 2008.

CLEANING BEIJING

In a showcase effort the government plans to clean up the capital city, Beijing, for the 2008 Olympic Games.

The city government plans to allocate 3 to 4 percent of its gross domestic product annually to control air pollution. Projects include switching from coal to natural gas, reducing traffic jams by constructing more new roads, and cutting industrial waste by setting up more waste treatment plants.

Planting and reforestation programs will add greenery in the urban districts and vegetation in the mountainous areas. The public, both households and businesses, will be urged to recycle waste, conserve energy and natural resources, and use public transportation.

AIR POLLUTION

Rapid industrialization has brought new wealth to China. Unfortunately, it has also led to increased industrial affluents. Many industrialized cities live under a layer of smog. To date, China is the second biggest emitter of carbon dioxide after the United States.

The industrial sector is the biggest source of carbon emissions because coal is still the major source of energy for businesses and homes. Coal-burning in China releases 650 million tons (650 billion kg) of carbon annually into the atmosphere.

Passengers cover their noses after alighting from a bus in Beijing. The city is a major industrial center and growing air pollution is a threat to agriculture and health.

WATER POLLUTION

Dumping industrial waste into waterways threatens the country's supply of drinking water. With the economy growing fast, controlling pollution will be difficult.

China will invest US$30 billion to deal with the problem of urban waste water between 2002 and 2010. The funds will be used to build waste water recycling plants, build better waste water disposal systems, and conduct research. Presently only 15 percent of waste water is treated.

To reduce pollution, new manufacturing plants must follow stricter emission standards. Factories in major Chinese cities such as Shanghai and Guangzhou have moved from city centers to industrial areas on the outskirts.

At the same time, old plants are required to upgrade their existing facilities to become environmentally friendly. Industries are also encouraged to develop other energy sources such as wind, geothermal, hydroelectric, and solar power.

NATURE CONSERVATION

In a country as vast as China, there are hundreds of thousands of species of wildlife, some facing extinction. The most famous is the giant panda.

Only about 1,000 of these endangered mammals are left, mainly in northern and northwestern Sichuan. The government launched a campaign in 1992 to protect these animals and their habitats from human encroachment and rampant logging. Other endangered animals in China include the golden monkey, black gibbon, Tibetan antelope, Siberian tiger, South China tiger, and Bactrian camel.

The southwestern provinces have some of the country's richest and most diverse vegetation. The region has 1,227 nature reserves covering 12 percent of China's total land area. To reduce the threat of erosion and flooding along major rivers, China banned logging near river banks in 1998 and has increased reforestation efforts.

Previously, many local governments took fertile agricultural land out of production in exchange for investments and economic growth. Stricter controls exist now to prevent that from happening again.

Above: **Panda bears Tian Tian and Mei Xiang in their new home at the National Zoo in Washington, D.C. On loan from China, they replaced the late Ling-Ling and Hsing-Hsing panda bears who had been at the zoo since 1972.**

Opposite: **Rubbish on the banks of the Yellow River in Yan'an, Shanxi Province. Government-led cleanup programs are targeting such areas.**

*A World Bank
report in August
2001 points to
three areas of
success in China's
recent effort
to tackle
environmental
damage and
pollution:
reducing
industrial air
and water
pollutant
emissions;
increasing
reforestation
and afforestation;
and reducing the
salinity caused
by pollution in
irrigation areas.*

WASTE MANAGEMENT AND RECYCLING

China creates at least 600 million tons (600 billion kg) of waste each year, and much of it is not properly treated. Of this, 155 million tons (155 billion kg) come from urban areas. To better manage waste and pollution, more money is needed and sound policies need to be implemented.

The Chinese government has received international praise for its efforts to manage waste and remedy ecological damage. It is also working to include sound environmental protection policies within the overall development strategy for the country.

For example, in 2000 China banned plastic foam dishware, which once rolled off 130 production lines across the nation, producing 10 billion units annually. The ban is part of China's commitment to phasing out ozone-depleting substances under various international agreements it has signed since the late 1980s. The government has formed an ozone layer protection group to identify projects that can be phased out to reduce the emissions that destroy the ozone layer.

INITIATIVES AND GOALS

China's Law on Environmental Protection was drafted in 1979 and passed by the National People's Congress in 1983. It made protecting the environment a basic national policy. Since then, the government has introduced additional measures to tackle environmental problems, which have become more complicated with development.

Education is one way to get the green message across. The first elementary school with environmental protection at the top of its teaching agenda will be established in Shanxi province, a coal-producing area. Businesses are urged to use environmentally friendly building materials

THREE GORGES DAM

Costing a total of US$25 billion, this 594-foot-high (181-m-high) dam on the Yangtze River will be the world's largest when completed in 2009. Strong foreign and domestic opposition to the construction state that it will uproot local culture, flood historical relics, and destroy the habitats

of endangered species of plants, animals, and fish. In addition, the project, which began in 1994, is plagued with corruption—contractors have skimped on equipment and pocketed the difference.

Because of the controversy surrounding the project, the United States has stayed clear of any involvement in it and has refrained from giving financial support to U.S. companies bidding for contracts. The World Bank has also decided not to fund the dam.

But the Chinese government and defenders of the dam expect the dam to eliminate the country's energy shortages, ensure cleaner air, and reduce the threat of flooding. Critics have been informed that the affected environment will be protected and the region's historical relics will be safe.

When completed, the dam will generate about 18 million kilowatts of power. It will have nearly 6 trillion gallons (23 trillion liters) of flood storage capacity that could cut the frequency of big downstream floods from once every 10 years to once every 100 years.

manufactured with energy-saving technology. The goal is to shrink energy use by 20 percent by 2005. Discharge of major water pollutants will be reduced by 10 percent by 2005. One of the biggest projects ever launched is the 10-year (2001–15) cleaning up of the Bohai Sea.

China has enlisted the help of international organizations such as the International Union for Conservation of Nature and Natural Resources (IUCNNR), the World Bank, and the United Nations on projects in its environmental protection programs, such as grassland reclamation in Inner Mongolia and protection of Tibetan antelopes.

CHINESE

MORE THAN 20 PERCENT of the world population lives in China. Population distribution in China is uneven; most people live along the fertile coastal areas, especially along the Yangtze River delta. Sichuan province has the most people at 114 million, or 445 persons per square mile (1,153 per square km); Tibet has the least at 2.6 million, or 4 persons per square mile (10 per square km). The cities are crowded, although 63 percent of the population live in the countryside—China has the largest number of farmers in the world.

HAN CHINESE

The Han, the largest ethnic group in China (1.2 billion people, or 92 percent of the population) and the world, originated around the Yellow, Yangtze, and Pearl rivers.

MINORITIES

The remaining 8 percent of China's population consists of 55 other ethnic groups. Found mostly along remote border regions around India, Afghanistan, Russia, Central Asia, and Vietnam, the biggest group is the Zhuang (15.5 million people) and the smallest is the Lloba (around 2,300 people).

Putonghua or Mandarin is the language of instruction in schools, but minorities are encouraged to teach their own languages and customs to their children.

There are almost nine million Manchus, mostly in northeastern China. They have their own script and language. China's rulers from 1644 to 1911, they have added to the richness of Chinese culture, including books written in Han Chinese.

Most of the 1.9 million Koreans live in northeastern China and in major cities. They have their own spoken and written language and their own newspapers. Koreans are fond of music and love to sing and dance at festivals.

Huis, at 8.6 million, are one of China's largest minorities. They are Muslims who live mainly in the northwest. Their customs are similar to those of Muslims in other countries. One outstanding Hui was the famous Ming Dynasty voyager Zheng He.

Kazakhs number 1.1 million and live mainly in Xinjiang in the northwest. They have their own script and are Muslims. Many Kazakhs live by animal husbandry, moving from place to place looking for pasture. They live in tents called *yurt*.

The 2,300 Llobas live in southeastern Tibet. Largely farmers, Llobas are also skilled at crafts. Hunting is important to them and young boys start early, joining adults in hunting trips. Staple foods include corn or millet dumplings.

The 6.6 million Yis live in southwestern China, in mountain areas, mainly as farmers. They have their own script and literature. Yi women live in their parents' home after marriage until their first child is born.

The one million Dais live in southern Yunnan province in southwestern China. Their staple food is rice, eaten with sour and hot dishes of fish, meats, and vegetables. Dais live in two-level houses built on stilts. Many Dais are Buddhists.

At 7.4 million, the Miaos are among the largest minorities in southwestern China. Miaos love to sing and their songs may be as long as 15,000 lines. They are also skilled craftsmen, although farming is the main occupation.

With 15.5 million people, Zhuangs are China's largest minority group. Most of them live in Guangxi in southwestern China. They are renowned for their singing. In the past, young people chose their mates at song festivals through songs.

The 19,000 Jings live in southwestern China's Guangxi province. They both fish and farm, the main crops being rice, sweet potatoes, peanuts, and millet. They read and write the Han script and speak Cantonese, having lived among the Han for a long time.

The 1.1 million Lis live on Hainan island. This southern tropical island is fertile, and the Lis may reap three crops of rice a year. Lis are known for their knowledge of herbal medicine. Li women are skilled in weaving and embroidery.

There are still other minority groups in China: the Drung, Jino, Hani, Lisu, Va, Naxi, Pumi, Blang, Nu, Lahu, Achang, and De'ang live in Yunnan province; the Bouyei, Dong, Shui, and Gelo live in Guizhou; the Mulam and Maonan live mainly in Guangxi; the She live in Fujian and Zhejiang; Mongolians, Daur, and Oroqen live throughout Inner Mongolia; Kirgiz, Xibe, and Tartar live mainly in Xinjiang; Bonan, Tu, Salar, and Yugur live mainly in Qinghai and Gansu; and Tibetans and Moinba live mainly in Tibet.

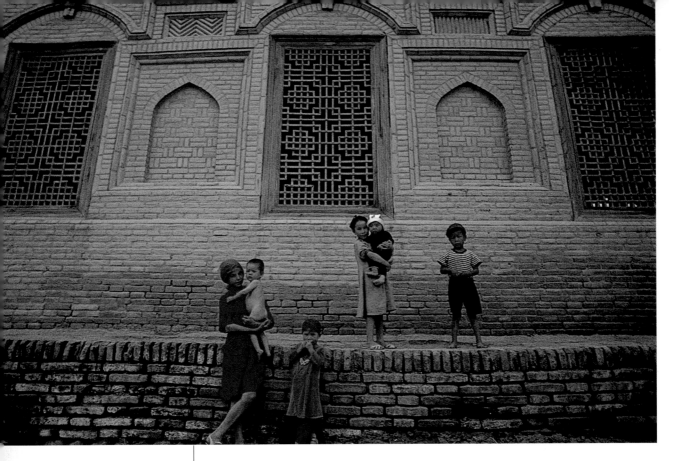

TIBETANS Surrounded on three sides by the highest mountains in the world, Tibet's remoteness and inaccessibility add to its mystery and fascination. It has a population of 4.6 million. Tibetans are a religious people and their life revolves around Lamaism, a form of Buddhism. Tibetans believe in reincarnation and the Dalai Lama, exiled by the Chinese government, is revered as a reincarnated Buddha-to-be.

Tibetans are a hospitable people. Their main occupation is farming and raising cattle. Their diet consists mainly of the grain they grow. Their favorite drink is *tsampa* ("sam-pa"), which is hot tea mixed with ground barley and yak butter.

UIGHUR Most of the 7.2 million Uighur live in Xinjiang province in northwestern China. They have settled in and around the oases of the Taklimakan Desert, cultivating fruit and grain and raising sheep and horses. The Uighur, who are Muslims, speak a language similar to Turkish and write in the Arabic script.

MONGOLIANS Mongolians number 4.8 million and are a nomadic people who live in the northern grasslands of Inner Mongolia. For most of the year, Mongolians move from place to place in search of new pastures for their cattle. They live in portable homes called *yurt,* ("yerht") which can be taken down and put up in another place.

The *yurt* is a tent made of animal hide, supported by strong wooden poles. The cylindrical walls are padded with thick felt to keep out the cold in winter. On the roof, skylights also act as air vents for warming fires. In summer, the base of the walls can be lifted up to let the cool breeze in.

In summer, Mongolians, whose main livelihood is raising cattle and horses, move around in search of grazing pastures. Their main diet consists of dairy products, meat, and grain. Vegetables, especially the leafy variety, are a rarity, so they eat mostly bean sprouts which can be grown anywhere in any season. Meat is often air-dried and it is often common to see strips of mutton hanging in and outside a *yurt*. Mongolians love tea boiled with milk from their cattle. Sometimes, butter-fried millet is added to it to improve the taste.

Mongolians are skilled horsemen and archers. They also enjoy wrestling, singing, and dancing. Television has entered the lives of these nomads, and in the evenings they can often be found in front of a television run by a generator outside their *yurt*.

Top: **Mongolian women in their tent.**

Above: **Mongolians in traditional dress.**

THE OVERSEAS CHINESE

Poverty, wars, and rebellions forced many Chinese to leave their country in search of a better life. Most left from provinces in southern China such as Guangdong, Fujian, and Shanghai. Some left for countries in nearby Southeast Asia such as Thailand, Malaysia, Singapore, and Indonesia; others went as far away as Europe, Africa, the Caribbean, South America, Australia, Canada, and the United States, where many settled in California to dig for gold or build railways.

Overseas Chinese, or *Hua Qiao* ("hu-ah chi-ow"), practice their own customs and traditions, some of which are not practiced by mainland Chinese. Although China is opening up, it still does not allow the free practice of certain customs and traditions.

The *Hua Qiao* community is large, numbering about 32 million. Many who made a better living overseas sent for their relatives. This is why we find large groups from a particular province in one country. California, for example, has a large Cantonese community, and Brazil has many Chinese from Fujian province.

The wish of some *Hua Qiao* is to go back to their home town. Many who have made good have returned to rebuild their ancestral home or make donations to build schools, hospitals, and public buildings in their villages or provinces.

POPULATION BOOM

China has always been a populous country. In an agricultural country, having more children means less work for each person. The Chinese also believe that the more sons one has, the better one will be looked after in old age. Also, the family name will be passed down to future generations.

With arable land so scarce in China, this huge population poses a great food problem. In the 1990s, the population grew at an annual average of about 1.1 percent, meaning there are about 14 million more mouths to feed each year. Another problem is housing, particularly in the cities where two or three generations live in a one-bedroom apartment. Improvements in health and a lower mortality rate have also contributed to the booming population.

FAMILY PLANNING

In 1982, family planning was made state policy. Late marriages and having fewer, healthier children were encouraged. City dwellers are now allowed to have only one child per couple, with penalties for having more children. However, couples with twins or triplets are not penalized. In rural areas, couples may have a second child, but must wait several years after the birth of the first child. Family planning also extends to the minority groups, but is not strictly enforced.

Family planning education starts young. "Puberty education" makes teenagers aware of their physical changes and of the correct attitude towards sex and marriage. When they grow up, they are taught about family planning before and after marriage.

In rural areas, where old customs still persist, the State Family Planning Commissioner teaches farmers about contraceptives and family planning.

LIFESTYLE

THE CHINESE ATTITUDE toward life is influenced by Confucian ethics, which teach respect and love for others.

PERSONAL RELATIONSHIPS

The Chinese make every effort not to embarrass another person, whether friend or foe. They do not openly reject a request or outwardly disagree with anything. They are brought up to mask their feelings, often by smiling or laughing. If someone responds to a request with "later" and later "forgets," it probably means that he or she cannot do the favor.

When two Chinese get to know each other, they establish *guanxi* ("KWAHNG-see"), or relationships. They are then obliged to exchange favors and never to reject requests, but to respond with "later" or "maybe."

The Chinese are also superb hosts. Tables remain filled with food even after dinner is through. To the Chinese, empty plates mean that their guests are still hungry and they have failed as hosts.

Chinese modesty does not allow them to accept flattery; instead they give it. Compliments are often brushed aside with an embarrassed laugh and a returned compliment.

Below: **A little chat and listening to birds singing.**

Opposite: **A mother carries her child on her back, freeing her hands for a snack.**

Song Dandan (*second woman from left*), a leading Chinese actress, picnics with several generations of her family and friends in the suburbs of Beijing.

FORMS OF ADDRESS

The Chinese have a title for every member of the household. This came about because historically the Chinese family was an extended one with several generations living under one roof.

The Chinese way of asking how many brothers and sisters one has is to ask how many older or younger siblings one has. Elder brothers are called *gege* ("keh-keh"), while younger ones are *didi* ("tee-tee"). *Jiejie* ("jee-eh-jee-eh") refers to elder sisters, while younger ones are called *meimei* ("may-may"). Different sets of names are given to each maternal and paternal grandparent and each aunt and uncle.

Outside the family, Chinese of all ages are known by their last name. Most of the time, *xiao* ("see-ow"), meaning little, is used as a prefix for younger people, and *lao* ("lah-ow"), meaning old, is put in front of the last name of a middle-aged person to show respect for his or her age and

THE CHINESE NAME

The Chinese name consists of three words: the family name comes first, then the generation name, and last the given name.

The family name is the proudest thing a Chinese inherits. It is by this name that a person is known outside the family.

The generation name denotes the generation in which a person is born. Often, brothers and male cousins share one generation name. There are no generation names for girls as the Chinese feel that girls belong to another family when they marry.

In rural villages where a whole community shares the same family name, there will be a book of generation names (*right*). It is possible to trace which generation a great-great-great grandfather belonged to by referring to this book.

Generation names are now less common as parents often have one child. Most children today just have a surname and the given name.

Parents often choose names that reflect virtues or talents they hope their children will possess. Feminine names such as Li, meaning beauty, or Fang, meaning fragrant, are common. Boys are given masculine names such as Qiang, meaning strength, and Wei, meaning greatness.

experience. These prefixes are used only for persons one is familiar with. In formal address, the last name is put before *xian sheng* ("si-an shehng"), or "Mr". Women keep their maiden names after marriage, replacing "Miss" with "Madam" behind their last names.

Teachers are well respected; *laoshi* ("LAH-OW-sheh"), meaning teacher, is always added after their last name. People in the streets address strangers as *tongzhi* ("TONG-sheh"), or comrade, when asking for directions or buying things.

THE EXTENDED FAMILY

In China, life revolves around the family. In the city, it is often common to find three generations living together under one roof, while in the countryside the family can extend to include uncles, aunts, cousins, and in-laws.

The oldest relative in the family is always respected as a person of wisdom whose word is usually law. The elderly are well looked after even if they are ill or bedridden. They are only sent to hospitals or institutions if the family cannot provide them with the proper care.

The greatest joy for the older generation is to see the whole family around them—the more males the better, as they are then assured that the family name will be carried on. The family hierarchy is carefully preserved, and each member of the family knows where he or she stands, even if the difference in age is only a few days. The younger generation is expected to not talk back or disobey orders from their elders.

Babies are well-loved in any Chinese family. With the one-child policy in China, the child is doted on and given almost everything he or she wants. In the extended family, the baby is certainly king.

Chinese women live with their parents until they marry. Once married, a woman stays with her husband in his home. The husband continues to live with his parents as it is his duty to look after them until their death.

GOING TO SCHOOL

Children start school at the age of six and a half. Urban children go to school for six full days a week. They get July and August off and four weeks vacation in the winter. There are four examinations a year.

The school day starts at 8 A.M. with four periods of 45 minutes each. There is a 10-minute break between periods and a two-hour break for

A grandmother with her grandchildren.

Playtime in school.

lunch. Afternoons are devoted to more lessons, homework, extracurricular activities, and doing chores around the school premises. The day ends at about 4:20 P.M.

After six years of elementary school, children go to high school. Among some of the subjects taught in high school are mathematics, a foreign language, politics, history, geography, sciences, music, and art. In the countryside, agricultural high schools can be found, where students are taught agricultural science and technology.

High school is divided into three years of junior high and three years of senior high education. Students can choose to pursue vocational training after junior high school. This prepares them for specialized jobs. Students who finish senior high school can take entrance examinations to universities or institutes that specialize in languages, research, teaching, or physical training.

Children in the countryside spend less time in the classroom. They help out in the fields during the planting and harvesting seasons. They go to schools near their farms, but they may have to walk two or three hours to school, starting at dawn.

Workers at a small paper mill. All workers in China and their families are looked after by their work unit.

THE ROLE OF THE WORK UNIT

A person's work unit, or *danwei* ("tahn-way"), might be a corporation or a small factory. Traditionally, the *danwei* looked after the welfare of its workers and their families from the day they started work until the day they died. However, the government is dismantling this system. Instead, people can choose their own jobs, and school graduates are no longer allocated jobs.

Workers now have to buy their own medical insurance and pay for their transportation and living expenses.

Many work units used to own apartment buildings for rental to their workers at a nominal rate. The government now encourages state workers to buy their own homes instead of waiting for housing allocation by their work unit. Under the home-ownership drive, many workers have bought apartments at a special discount given by the government.

Although the significance of the work unit has diminished, the *danwei* is still outwardly responsible for the individual worker. For instance, it

WOMEN IN CHINA

The women of ancient China were essentially homebound and their social behavior highly controlled. Girls had their feet bound when they were between 4 and 8 years old to stop their feet from growing.

This painful process, which was considered a beauty treatment, left them with small misshapen, club-like feet as they grew older. With tiny feet supporting their weight, they could just manage small steps at a time. Still, their gait like "a swaying willow tree," was considered attractive and kept them from venturing too far from home. The practice continued until well into the 20th century.

After China became a republic, the status of Chinese women was officially equal to men. Women played a big part in rebuilding China. Most took on jobs once only held by men, such as doctors, engineers, factory workers, soldiers, and even jobs involving manual labor, such as farmers and porters.

Women are now an important part of the workforce. They have equal pay with men and carry the same workload. Many Chinese men share responsibilities for their children and do household chores like cooking, cleaning, and ironing.

Women are well-represented in the government and hold key positions in large organizations. It is felt that if anyone can do a job, that person should be given the responsibility regardless of gender.

must officially give approval for a couple intending to get married. Likewise, if they are thinking of divorce, the *danwei* tries to help them reconcile, if possible.

Overseas travel requires approval by the work unit. Before, Chinese could travel only on official business or on a scholarship, but they can now travel in tour groups to selected foreign countries for pleasure. A growing number have gone overseas for higher education or work.

In theory, a Chinese worker cannot be fired. So factories send their workers home but still keep them on the payroll, providing them with a basic monthly living allowance. Before a worker can switch jobs, the *danwei* must sign the release paper.

Below: **Newlyweds in the city usually hold a dinner for family and friends. But it is increasingly popular for them to spend their money on a honeymoon or new home. If so, they announce their wedding by treating family and friends to some candy.**

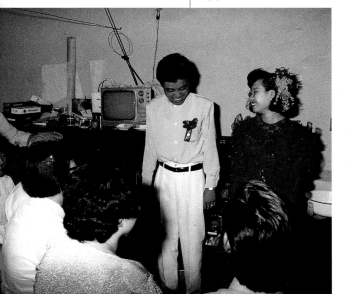

Opposite: **Mother and child are confined to the home during the first month after birth. On the day the child is one month old, a celebration is held, after which the mother is said to be fit enough for normal work.**

MARRIAGE

Traditionally, marriages were elaborate events with days of feasting and complicated rites. The wedding day would be the first time the bride and groom actually set eyes on each other as marriages were prearranged by parents.

Nowadays, couples choose their marriage partners, but must seek the approval of their *danwei*. If approval is given, they can register their marriage. This is a simple civil ceremony, after which they may arrange a celebration. Usually, an auspicious date will be picked. A popular date is the seventh day of the seventh moon. According to an old story this is the only day that a fairy from heaven gets to meet her mortal husband.

Autumn months are popular for weddings, as the weather is good and the moon is at its brightest. In the country, the winter months are good for weddings, as work on the farm is relatively slow and time can be spent cooking a feast for the whole village.

Before the wedding day, the groom's family buys electrical appliances such as a refrigerator for the couple's new home and a trousseau and jewelry for the bride.

On the wedding day, the groom makes his way to the bride's house in a bus hired for the occasion. The bride and groom are dressed in new everyday clothes, though many brides now wear the white wedding gown. The couple go to the groom's house where the bride will meet her new family and the celebrations begin.

CHILDBIRTH

There is often great excitement when a wife conceives. The expectant mother is well looked after and well fed. Chinese mothers usually hold full-time jobs and continue to work until the seventh month of pregnancy, when they are given lighter tasks. In the city, mothers are by law given three months of paid maternity leave.

Customs concerning childbirth are more prevalent in the countryside than in the city. Pregnant women are not allowed to join in any social occasions, especially weddings and funerals, from the start of pregnancy to 100 days after the child is born.

There are more taboos after birth, perhaps because some homes are far from medical facilities. Women are not allowed to bathe, wash their hair, or do any household chores for one month after the birth of their child.

During this time, the mother regains her strength with plenty of rest and good food. Fresh, uncooked fruit and vegetables are avoided as they are believed to be too *yin* ("yin"), meaning cooling, to the system and may cause the mother to fall ill. The mother's diet consists mainly of noodles, eggs, and chicken. Fresh anchovies are often made into a soup, as this is believed to increase the production of breast milk for the newborn.

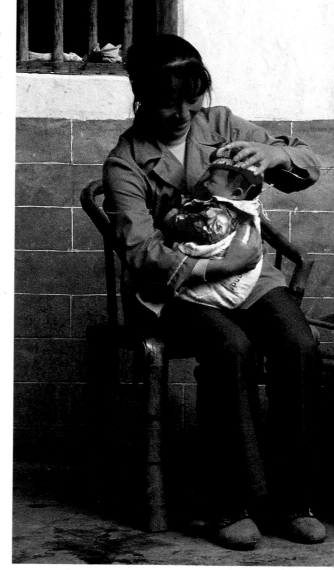

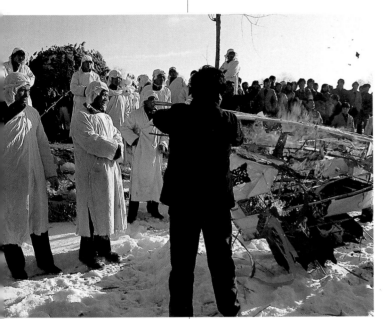

Paper objects represen-
ting money, clothes, and
other possessions are
burned at the funeral, so
that the deceased will be
well provided for in the
"yellow spring," or the
afterlife.

DEATH

When a person dies, his or her *danwei* is informed and officials are sent to see if they can help in any way with the funeral arrangements and pay for certain funeral expenses.

The body is taken to the nearest crematorium, bathed, and dressed in funeral clothes. It is then placed in a glass coffin for friends and family to pay their last respects before cremation. After cremation, the ashes are placed in a special box and put in the crematorium or taken home.

In the countryside, where burial is more common than cremation, people make their own elaborately decorated coffins. Preparations for death start when a person is still alive. Once people reach 50 years or so, they or their children will start making a coffin. Once it is finished, it is stored in the house until the time of death. It may sound morbid, but people are happy to know that their children will carry out the last rites.

Death rites in the countryside start with a wake that can last up to one week. Friends and relatives come from near and far to partake in a feast and pay their last respects. The family of the deceased wear white hoods and robes. Sacrificial items like paper money, paper houses, and paper cars are burned to make sure the deceased will be comfortable in the afterlife. The coffin is then buried on the family's land.

The government is trying to discourage burial in favor of cremation.

CHINESE HOMES

Country houses are spacious. They are often part of walled compounds, with a simple wooden door opening into a courtyard. On either side of the courtyard is a kitchen and a storeroom or extra bedroom. Facing the entrance is the main hall, consisting of the living room and one or two bedrooms. There is often a water pipe in the kitchen and another in the courtyard. Toilet facilities are found outside the house and are shared by two or three families.

In the city, similar houses are very cramped; three or four families may share a common courtyard. More fortunate urbanites live in hard-to-get apartments with a kitchen, living room, bedroom, and toilet. Homes seldom have bathrooms; often the only source of water is at the kitchen sink. Shower facilities are provided by most companies on their premises for their staff. In addition, there are public baths. The multi-function living room is used to entertain guests, have meals, and at night, serves as an extra bedroom.

Every available space is used for storage. It is common to see boxes of belongings stacked on cupboards, under beds, and along corridors. Even window sills are put to good use for storing or drying food for the winter.

As standards of living improve and with government encouragement, home-buying is becoming fashionable with the middle class in Shanghai, Guangzhou, and Beijing.

An apartment block in Guangxi. Chinese homes are often dimly lit to save energy. In cities, power shortages are a problem: there is often one day a week without electricity.

TRADITIONAL CHINESE DRESS

Most Chinese wear Western-style clothes. Adults own at least one Mao-style suit. Usually made of thick, dark blue cotton, it is a simple tunic with buttons down the front.

The Mao-style suit made its appearance when China became a republic; it was first used as a uniform in the army. Later it became widely used even by civilians because its simple design and tough fabric was practical in lean times when all people needed was something warm and lasting.

Women also took to wearing Mao-style suits. Before the Cultural Revolution, women wore the cheongsam, a long slim dress with a modest slit up the side, to formal functions. This feminine dress was later discouraged, but it has since made a comeback among women in the city.

THE RED SCARF

A red scarf is worn around the neck by elementary school children (*right*). The scarf represents a corner of the Chinese flag and is worn by members of the Young Pioneers League, a junior section of the Communist Party.

The scarf is formally presented to the children in a ceremony. The children later choose whether or not they want to join the Communist Party's Youth League.

TRADITIONAL CHINESE MEDICINE

Traditional Chinese medicine has its origins in the countryside, where people discovered by trial and error that combinations of certain herbs relieved certain ailments. Books listing herbs and their functions were written as far back as the Han Dynasty.

A Chinese pharmacy stocks and dispenses traditional medicine. Rows and rows of wooden drawers cover the walls in the pharmacy, each containing a kind of herb. Prescriptions are made up by combining several kinds of herbs. There is usually a doctor of Chinese medicine in attendance. By taking the patient's pulse, looking at the color of the tongue and skin, and noting other symptoms, the doctor can diagnose the problem. A simple headache can be linked to organs such as the liver or kidney that are temporarily under stress and not functioning well. Medicine is prescribed to relieve the headache and a tonic recommended to get the organ back to normal. As herbs are slow-acting, they have to be taken over a long period of time.

Traditional Chinese medicine is taken not just to relieve a symptom or cure an illness but also to improve bodily functions. Brews of herbs, leaves, bark, and berries are cooked for hours before being consumed. Sometimes more exotic ingredients such as animal horns, dried snakes and lizards, and the fat glands of the Manchurian snow frog are added for a more potent brew.

Besides herbal medicine, traditional medical treatment includes massage, deep-breathing exercises, and acupuncture.

ACUPUNCTURE Acupuncture is based on the Chinese theory that the body has a network of energy lines known as meridians. These meridians are linked and they affect the major organs of the body. According to the theory, when a person is not feeling well, it is thought that there is an imbalance of *yin* and *yang* ("young") or an uneven distribution of *qi* ("chi"), meaning "energy" or "force."

Along the meridians are certain points where needles are placed to get the *qi* ("chi"), to flow again. Different-sized needles

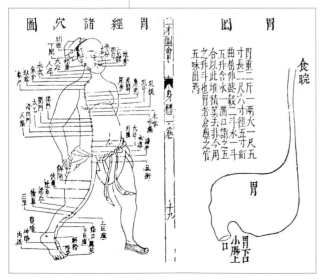

An acupuncture chart from the *Wei Jing*, or *Treatise on the Stomach,* from a Chinese encyclopedia of the early 17th century.

YIN AND YANG

In Taoist belief, the human body holds two intertwining forces, *yin* and *yang*. *Yin* is represented by femininity, darkness, cold, and water. *Yang* is masculinity, sun, heat, and fire. These forces are symbolized as black and white respectively (*right*).

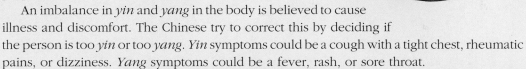

This does not mean that a female possesses only *yin* qualities. A very active girl who is always perspiring and prone to fevers and sore throats is thought to be more *yang* than *yin*, so her mother will feed her more foods with *yin* properties.

An imbalance in *yin* and *yang* in the body is believed to cause illness and discomfort. The Chinese try to correct this by deciding if the person is too *yin* or too *yang*. *Yin* symptoms could be a cough with a tight chest, rheumatic pains, or dizziness. *Yang* symptoms could be a fever, rash, or sore throat.

If the discomfort is not serious, home cures in the form of a special food included in a meal could relieve a patient. Food falls into three categories: hot, cooling, and neutral. For example, cucumber, watercress, and fruit are cooling, while garlic, peppers, and chives are hot.

Chinese medicine and diet regulate the body system and bring the body to its original equilibrium.

are used to pierce the skin at varying angles and depths. They are then twirled or vibrated by hand or electronically until a numbing sensation is felt. It is this sensation that the acupuncturist is aiming for to relieve the ailment.

There are over 300 acupuncture points throughout the body. In the course of treating an ailment, it is common practice to stick needles in the ears, on the face and neck, and in between the fingers and toes.

Like traditional Chinese herbal medicine, acupuncture should be carried out over a period of time to be fully effective.

Acupuncture is most commonly used as an anaesthetic in China and in other countries. With acupuncture, even major surgery can be performed with the patient fully conscious and feeling no pain at all.

RELIGION

TO MOST CHINESE, religion is a mixture of various Chinese philosophies. Apart from the Christians and Muslims, most other Chinese practice a mixture of Taoist, Confucian, and Buddhist beliefs.

Taoism, Confucianism, and Buddhism began as philosophies. Their teachings relate to living in harmony with nature. They later became popular religions and were intermingled by the Chinese so that, for example, a Taoist could have Confucian and Buddhist beliefs as well.

Chinese are generally superstitious, the result of the Taoist belief of keeping in harmony with nature and the universe. To ensure good luck in major events such as marriage or moving to new premises, people appeal to the gods' goodwill by choosing an auspicious date and time on the lunar calendar, when the moon is full or when zodiac signs do not clash. Firecrackers are set off to scare away offending spirits, and red is used almost everywhere to attract good fortune.

The Chinese authorities, however, disapprove of too much superstition, believing that it inhibits one's thinking and actions. The younger generation is less superstitious than those born in pre-communist times (before 1949).

Although the constitution of 1982 guarantees religious freedom, the majority of Chinese are atheists, as most grew up during the Cultural Revolution when religious groups were persecuted.

TAOISM

Taoism teaches humans to live in harmony with nature. Taoists believe in supernatural beings, use charms and spells, meditate, and keep to a vegetarian diet. They believe that these practices can help them gain immortality and be one with the universe. Taoism was founded by the philosopher Lao Zi whose name means "old master."

Above: **A statue of Chinese philosopher Confucius.**

Opposite: **The Lokapala, one of many deities worshiped by the Chinese.**

CONFUCIANISM

Born in 551 B.C., Confucius was a government official who became a teacher of moral philosophy later in life. His philosophy became the backbone of Chinese thinking and behavior.

Confucius lived in a time of political violence and social disorder. He devoted his life to the teaching of *ren* ("rehn") or the love of humankind. Linked to this is *xiao* ("si-ow"), or filial piety, devotion to one's parents. Ancestor worship ensures that this devotion continues after the death of the parents. Tablets bearing the name of the deceased are kept in homes, and the deceased are honored and remembered especially on their birthdays and death anniversaries.

Other qualities connected with *ren* are loyalty, courage, wisdom, and trustworthiness. The aim of cultivating such qualities is to become a superior person. Confucianism also encouraged interest in the arts to stimulate the mind.

BUDDHISM

Buddhism was brought to China along the Silk Road by Indian merchants. By the sixth century it was established as a major religion in China. Chinese monks journeyed to India and Sri Lanka to bring back Sanskrit scriptures and sutras to be translated into Chinese. The recorded journeys of traveling monks have become important historical literature. In China, the Buddhist philosophy absorbed Taoist and Confucian ideas. In Tibet, Buddhism blended with Bon, an indigenous ancient religion of Tibet to become Lamaism.

ISLAM

Islam came into China via Arab and Persian merchants around the seventh century. Scholars and missionaries arrived and mosques were built. The integration of Islam with Chinese society is seen in the way Muslims have changed their names to Chinese surnames: Muhammad, Mustafa, and Masoud have become Mo, Mai, and Mu.

A Tibetan Lama Buddhist monk.

CHRISTIANITY

The earliest Christians to arrive in China, in A.D. 735, were the Nestorian Christians from Syria. In the 13th century, the Jesuits came and brought with them sciencific knowledge. When China opened up to the world after the Opium Wars, Protestant and Roman Catholic missionaries arrived. Although Christian missionaries opened schools, universities, and hospitals, Christianity never became a popular religion in China.

The Kai Yuan Temple in Fujian province. Images of the Buddha fill the main prayer hall.

THE CHINESE TEMPLE

The Chinese temple is a fascinating place. Its halls are filled with statues of gods and demigods. Some of these are celestial beings, others are mythical characters, and some are individuals elevated from the status of mere mortals because of their brave or outstanding feats.

A pair of door gods, usually stone lions, guard the main entrance. They are said to have guarded a passage used by spirits a long, long time ago. Wicked spirits were weeded out by the door gods and then bound and fed to tigers. It became a tradition to paint the door gods' images on temple doors to scare away evil spirits who might want to slip in.

Inside the temple, incense and paper offerings are burned in the courtyard. Offerings of food and drink are made at the altar in the main hall. The fragrance of joss, or incense, sticks fills the air, and candles and oil lamps light the dim interior. Worshipers give thanks for wishes granted or pray for blessings for a better life.

WIND AND WATER

Feng shui ("fehng shu-ay"), or wind and water, is the practice of living in harmony with the natural environment for good fortune and health. It was first practiced in ancient China by farmers, to whom wind and water were very important natural forces that could either destroy or nurture their crops.

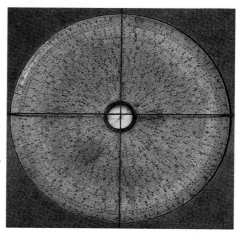

Today, *feng shui* has developed into the art of locating buildings and other manmade structures such as fountains and bridges to harmonize with and benefit from the surrounding physical environment.

The Chinese believe that there are invisible forces beneath the earth—positive *yang* and negative *yin*. A compass called a *luopan* ("lu-ow-pahn") measures these forces. Balancing the two forces in a person's immediate surroundings is important for good health and fortune. For example, warm colors representing the positive force in a room should be balanced by cool colors representing the negative force.

A building ideally should be situated with a hill protecting the back of the building and calm water in front for a soothing view. A huge tree that shadows the main entrance could prevent fortune from entering, while a swift flowing drain or river nearby could carry all the luck away. Doors are sometimes built at an angle to prevent bad luck from entering, and mirrors are hung above doors or windows to scare away evil spirits with their own reflections.

A popular goddess is Guan Yin ("Kwahn Yin"), who can manifest herself in thousands of forms. Also known as the Goddess of Mercy, she is said to be sympathetic to her followers and to help them in times of trouble.

In every nook and cranny of the temple, deities representing health, wealth, and longevity and images of the Buddha are found. The most popular Buddha figure is the bald, smiling Buddha with a protruding belly. He is a favorite as his disposition represents wealth, joy, and long life.

LANGUAGE

CHINA HAS A WEALTH of languages. Besides Putonghua (Mandarin), the common language, eight major dialects are spoken across different regions. These dialects vary from one province to another and even from village to village.

MAJOR DIALECTS

The northern dialect or Bei Fang Hua forms the basis of Putonghua, China's official language, and is spoken by Chinese living in the northern, central, and southwestern provinces. More than 70 percent of the Chinese population speak this dialect.

The Wu dialect is spoken by people around Shanghai, Jiangsu, and Zhejiang provinces. Xiang is spoken in Hunan province, the Gan dialect is spoken in Jiangxi and Hubei provinces, and Keija (Hakka) is spoken in parts of Guangdong, Fujian, and Jiangxi provinces.

The northern Min dialect is spoken in parts of Fujian and Taiwan, while southern Min is spoken in southern Fujian, parts of Hainan, most of Taiwan, and by many overseas Chinese. Another dialect spoken by many overseas Chinese and throughout Guangdong and southeastern Guangxi province is Yue (Cantonese).

The written form of all Chinese dialects is the same. So while a northerner may not be able to communicate verbally in dialect with a southerner, they can read each other's writing.

Above: **Tête-á-tête— Chinese from different regions speak different dialects.**

Opposite: **The Chinese all share a common script.**

The language of instruction in Chinese schools is Putonghua, or Mandarin.

PUTONGHUA

China is united by a common tongue, Putonghua, also known as Mandarin. Putonghua is derived from a northern Chinese dialect. Since 1949, Putonghua has been taught in schools across China.

The Chinese language is the oldest continuously used language in the world today. It also has more speakers than any other language in the world. Spoken Chinese has 400 sounds but 40,000 to 50,000 characters or words in written form. The limited number of sounds is made up for by variation in tones.

There are four tones in Putonghua. The four tones used to distinguish words are:

- high and level (as in *High* Noon)
- rising (as in asking "Here?")
- falling and rising (as in asking "*May* I... ?")
- high and falling (as in exclaiming "No!" in an argument)

The same word said in a different tone can have different meanings. For example:

"*Ni you bing* [first tone] *ma?*" ("nee yo ping mah") means "Do you have some ice?"

"*Ni you bing* [third tone] *ma?*" means "Do you have a cookie?"

"*Ni you bing* [fourth tone] *ma?*" means "Are you ill?"

MINORITY LANGUAGES

The 55 minorities of China, some of which have subgroups, speak their own languages. The four main minority language groups are Altaic, Tibeto-Burmese, Tai, and Miao-Yao.

The Altaic language group includes the Turkic languages spoken by the Uighur and Kazakhs in Xinjiang and the dialects of the Mongolians in Inner Mongolia. The Tibetans, Yi, and Tujia, who live mainly in the west and southwest, speak Tibeto-Burmese languages.

Hill people in southern Sichuan and certain parts of Yunnan also speak Tibeto-Burmese languages. The Tai language group is spoken by a large number of minorities in Guangxi, Yunnan, and Guizhou. The Miao and Yao languages are closely related to each other and belong to the Sino-Tibetan family.

After 1949, institutes specializing in the research and development of minority languages were set up. One of their aims was to help minorities develop their own written script using the Latin alphabet.

Lessons for minority children are conducted in Putonghua, but the school curriculum also includes lessons in their home language. Minority languages are used locally in books, newspapers, and magazines. Radio and television programs in major minority languages such as Mongolian, Tibetan, Uighur, Kazakh, and Korean are aired daily.

Nu women dressed in their best clothes are on their way to celebrate the Torch Festival. The Nu, who live in Yunnan province, speak a language belonging to the Tibeto-Burmese group, which has no written form. Few minority languages have their own script.

The development of Chinese characters through the centuries. The earliest known version is on the left, while on the right are words which have been in use since after A.D. 200. The top row of characters represents the sun, the second row the moon, the third row a vehicle, and the fourth row a horse.

THE WRITTEN LANGUAGE

There are about 50,000 characters in the Chinese script, of which only 3,000 are in common use. It is not surprising that no one knows all the characters.

Developed about 6,000 years ago, Chinese characters are among the oldest form of written language in the world. The Chinese first started expressing their ideas in drawings. Sometimes whole pictures were drawn and sometimes just the outline or representative part of an idea was used. These pictures and outlines are known as ideographs. Take for example "sun" 日, "sheep" 羊 , and "horse" 马.

In the early stages, one ideograph represented just one word. As more words were introduced, two or more ideographs were combined to form new ideographs. For example, the ideograph for "combine" 合 and the ideograph for "hand" 手 together mean "to take" 拿. Sometimes words express whole ideas. Take for example *xiuxi* ("si-yoo-si") meaning "rest" 休息: "man" 人 under a "tree" 木 resting his "eyes" 目 and "heart" 心.

There are 11 basic strokes, and Chinese characters are written in a proper sequence. Written out of sequence, the word often loses its form and proportion. Children, when first learning how to write, practice for hours drawing dots, dashes, and strokes. They soon learn how to decipher the sequence in which to write a word they see for the first time. The simplest word has only one stroke while the most complicated has 30.

The Chinese take their handwriting seriously, as it reflects their character and upbringing. Often, one's handwriting is a deciding factor in whether the letter will be read or put aside for consideration. People of high standing often have very distinctive handwriting and are often

Che Che Café, or Vehicle Café, in Kunming. *Che* is the pinyin form of 车, meaning "vehicle."

privileged to put their handwriting on important signs or letterheads. There is even a restaurant in Beijing displaying an example of an emperor's handwriting because he stopped by one night and enjoyed the dumplings.

In 1964, the Chinese government introduced a form of simplified words. These have fewer strokes than the original word but keep the basic shape and meaning. For example, the word "bird," originally written as 鳥, is now written as 鸟.

In an attempt to make Mandarin more intelligible to the Western world, a system known as *pinyin* ("pin-yin") was developed. The system phonetically translates Chinese words into Romanized script.

CHINESE IDIOMS

In everyday conversation, the Chinese sprinkle their speech with idioms and puns. Using the correct idiom at the right time is appreciated as a sign of culture or wit.

Some idioms are fairly straightforward, such as *lao ma shi tu* ("lah-ow mah sheh tu"), meaning "an old horse knows the road." Others may not make sense unless one knows the story behind the saying. For example, *hua she tian zu* ("hu-ah sheh ti-ahn zhu"), meaning "to draw a snake and add feet to it," describes someone who has already completed something and spoils it all by overdoing things.

The story behind the snake saying is as follows: There were some men who discovered a jar of wine that held enough only for one person to drink. They decided to hold a contest to see who could draw a snake in the sand. The fastest one got to drink the wine. The man who finished first had so much time to spare that he added feet to his snake. Then he snatched up the wine jar, claiming it was his as he had finished first. The man who finished next insisted that although his friend had indeed finished first, there was no such thing as a snake with feet, so the wine rightfully belonged to him.

"Guarding the tree and waiting for the hare."

HOW TO COUNT TO TEN ON ONE HAND

The Chinese have a way of indicating the numbers one to 10 using only the fingers on one hand. It is very useful at busy and noisy marketplaces where signing may be more effective than shouting the number of oranges one wants to buy.

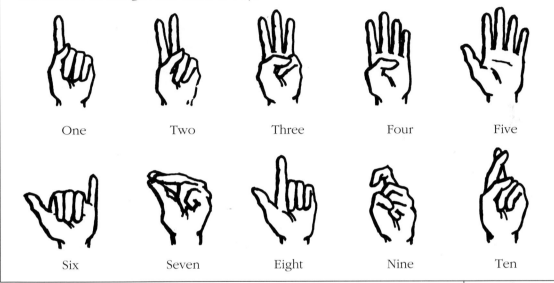

| One | Two | Three | Four | Five |

| Six | Seven | Eight | Nine | Ten |

Shou zhu dai tu ("show zhu tie too"), meaning "guarding the tree and waiting for the hare," describes one who leaves things to chance. In the story, a farmer saw a hare running so fast that it crashed into a tree and broke its neck. The farmer happily had it for dinner that night and went to the same spot the next day to wait for another hare to do the same thing.

Another saying is *ba miao zhu zhang* ("pa meow zhu chang"), meaning "to pull the shoots to help it to grow," is a lesson for those who are impatient. There was a farmer who thought his rice plants were taking a long time to grow, so he pulled the new shoots upward. Then he looked at them with satisfaction for the shoots were indeed taller. He went home to tell his family what he had done. Later when his family went to see what he had done, they found a field of dead plants.

ARTS

MANY STYLES OF ART in China developed during the Tang Dynasty when artistic expression reached a sophisticated level.

DECORATIVE ART

Chinese decorative art captures symbols of nature and myth on fabric, porcelain, ceramics, and other materials.

Around the seventh century, a white clay was discovered along the banks of the Yellow and Yangtze Rivers. This clay produced white porcelain pieces that became so refined that they were eggshell thin and translucent. Perhaps the most popular of these are the blue and white Ming porcelain pieces. They became so famous in the West that they were called "china," after their place of origin.

Another colorful art form is cloisonné. Enamel paint, blue being the most popular, is used to fill in thin plates which are then soldered onto metal bases. A skill brought to China from Persia during the Ming Dynasty, cloisonné decorates everything from grandfather clocks to chopsticks.

The Chinese also refined the art of carving. They usually carve jade or ivory, using special knives as small as toothpicks to create the fine details.

An opera stage uses simple props. Sometimes it has painted canvas backdrops representing a hall, garden, or palace. A small orchestra takes up one wing of the stage.

p 88: A dough doll maker. Dough dolls are made of flour dough and last as long as the weather is cold.

p 89: Ceramics for sale.

OPERA

This classic form of entertainment started out as street performances where gongs, cymbals, and drums were used to attract the audience. This "cacophony" is still the trademark of Chinese opera and marks the start of each new scene.

Each region has its own style of opera. Some stress singing, others acrobatics or dancing. Sung in the local dialects, operas are still performed as outdoor entertainment.

The most popular style of Chinese opera comes from Beijing; it originated 200 years ago. It took the best aspects of the different styles from other parts of China and integrated them into a style that includes singing, dancing, mime, and acrobatics.

The operas tell stories from historical epics, folk legends, classical novels, and fairy tales. Lines are sung in classical Chinese with lyrics flashed by the side of the stage so the audience can follow the story or sing along, which they often do. Accompanying music is provided by an orchestra that includes Chinese fiddles, flutes, wooden clappers, lutes, drums, cymbals, and gongs.

THE MONKEY KING

The Monkey King, or Sun Wukong, is probably the best-loved character in Chinese opera. There are between 500 and 600 operas that revolve around his adventures and antics. Most of these stories are based on the novel *Journey to the West* written by Wu Chang'en in the 16th century.

Sun Wukong, a celestial being, accompanies his master, a Buddhist monk, to India in search of religious scriptures. Along the way he endures all kinds of dangers and hardships and protects his master from demons and evil beings.

Totally devoted to his master, he is a clever, cunning, and disobedient character with a good heart. His monkey-like antics and mischief amuse audiences of all ages.

Most operas about Sun Wukong are filled with acrobatics. Somersaults, tumbles, and falls make up most of the spectacular fighting scenes. Actors who play the Monkey King spend their whole careers perfecting the art and are able to imitate the actions and characteristics of the monkey.

Chinese literature, which includes operatic drama, has a 3,000-year history and is one of the major literary heritages of the world. It has greatly influenced the literary traditions of other Asian countries, particularly Korea, Japan, and Vietnam. These countries have adopted the Chinese script as part of their written language.

An evening at the opera can be a three- or four-hour affair. Whole families turn up for performances, and the atmosphere in the theater is rowdy and almost festive, with drinks and dried melon seeds passed around. Shouts of *"hao!"* ("how"), meaning "good," punctuate solo performances and exciting combat scenes. Spectators who stand up and join in the chorus are sometimes as entertaining as the actors. Chinese love the opera and often one finds old men walking in the streets, transistor radios held to their ears, listening intently to an opera.

OPERA PARAPHERNALIA

There are four major roles in each opera. The *sheng* ("shehng") or male lead is either an older man or a military or civilian hero, who is almost always strong, handsome, and intelligent. *Dan* ("dun") characters are female leads who are dignified, virtuous women, younger women who are witty and charming, or military heroines. The *jing* ("ching"), or *dahualian* ("ta-hu-ah-li-an"), meaning "big painted face," is a male actor with a painted face emphasizing his strength or social standing. *Chou* ("chow"), or *xiaohualian* ("si-ow-hu-li-an"), meaning "small painted face," is the clown. He lends comic relief to the more serious scenes. These lead players are distinguished by the costumes they wear and their stage makeup.

The *sheng,* or male lead, here a military hero (as indicated by the pheasant feather on his headdress) who is also a scholar (indicated by the water sleeves).

Heavily embroidered and in dazzling colors, opera costumes liven up a relatively bare stage. Military heroes wear padded armor and splendid headdresses with long pheasant feathers. Men and women wear fluid robes with long "water" sleeves, which they use for effect in flirting, crying, and in showing fear and anger.

Stage makeup is as fascinating as the costumes. Actors paint their faces according to the roles they play. Red represents loyalty and uprightness. White is for slyness and treachery. Yellow is for craftiness or cleverness. Blue and green represent evil spirits, while silver and gold color the face of gods and fairies. Heroes and heroines usually have simple white- and pink-based faces with exaggerated eye makeup. Regular theatergoers are able to identify characters by their makeup.

ACROBATICS

This performing art is 22 centuries old in China. It started out as a means of livelihood for farmers during the winter months and developed into one of the most popular forms of entertainment in China and abroad.

Props used are often household items like dishes and furniture. These objects are often tossed in the air or piled precariously one on top another. Balancing acts on bicycles, piles of chairs (*right*), or large urns are common, and so are contortionist acts.

Acrobatic acts often include performing animals.

Acrobats are so popular that there are acrobatic troupes that represent towns or large associations. At present, there are over 120 acrobatic troupes at county level and above, involving more than 12,000 performers.

In the past 40 years, many Chinese acrobatic troupes have toured more than 100 countries to promote friendship and cultural exchanges.

Props may only be a table and two chairs against a painted canvas backdrop. The audience has to exercise its imagination to follow the story. One flag carried by a soldier represents a thousand men, two flags with wheels painted on them are a chariot, and a flag with appropriate characters written on it may indicate a flood or strong winds. Actors who jump off chairs are trying to drown themselves in rivers or wells, while those climbing tables and chairs are crossing hills and mountain ranges.

Training for the opera is rigorous and actors start when they are as young as 10 years old.

CALLIGRAPHY

Chinese calligraphy is more than handwriting—it is an art. A well-written piece conjures up images of strength, beauty, or grace. Characters can look graceful and feminine or strong and masculine, even vigorous, forceful, hot, or cold. Calligraphers write poems, couplets, or proverbs, which are hung on the walls.

The Chinese place great importance on good calligraphy, and from the Tang to the Qing dynasties a scholar's handwriting carried great weight in his score on the civil service examination. Poets take as much pride in the writing as in the content of their poems.

Calligraphy on stone by Wang Xizhi, representing the earliest evolution of the "regular script," or *kai shu*.

There are several forms of calligraphy. One is a formal style with regular characters that are angular, with no circles and few curved lines. Then there is the *cao shu* ("chao shu"), or grass style, thus named because writing in this style appears as if the wind has blown over the grass. Only those who have studied calligraphy for a long time can decipher words written in this style. Another style is the *kai shu* ("khai shu"), developed 2,000 years ago but still used by the Chinese today as regular writing.

The tools for Chinese calligraphy are few—brush, ink stick, ink stone, and paper (sometimes silk). These are known as the four treasures of calligraphy.

PAINTING

Chinese painting involves five subjects: human figures, landscapes, flowers, birds and animals, and fish and insects. Paintings are usually done on silk or absorbent paper made of bamboo pulp. A pointed brush is used

A painter at work. The bamboo is one of four plants that make up one branch of Chinese painting. The other three plants are the orchid, plum, and chrysanthemum. The bamboo symbolizes the strength of character of a moral person.

to apply paint made of mineral and plant pigments. Color, if used at all, is applied in small amounts for a washed look.

Chinese paintings strive to catch the spirit of the subject. Artists sometimes meditate before picking up the brush and in a burst of energy put an image to paper. Works are painted from memory and executed quickly and confidently. Unlike Western art, a picture is completed within minutes, and an artist may paint the same subject again and again until the desired effect is achieved. Many famous artists specialize in painting just one subject, such as birds, insects, shrimp, or even donkeys.

Brush strokes are important as they contribute to the texture of the painting. They are given fancy names like "rain drops," "ax cuts," or "wrinkles on a devil's face." Calligraphy is almost always used to complete a Chinese painting. A couplet or poem complements the picture.

Finger painting started in the Tang Dynasty and is regarded as a high art form. The fingernails are the main tools. They are kept long and well shaped, as a broken nail hinders the artist.

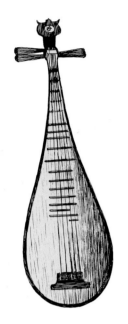

MUSICAL INSTRUMENTS

When Emperor Qin Shihuang ordered all books to be burned, most musical instruments were destroyed as well. What we see today are mostly tribal instruments that were adapted or adopted by the Hans to make music. Below are some instruments found in a Chinese orchestra.

ERHU ("erh-who")   A fiddle with two strings played with a bow made of bamboo and horse hair. The *erhu* usually has a cylindrical sound box made of wood or bamboo. Animal hide such as sheep or snake skin is stretched over one of its sides, creating different qualities of sound. Some of these fiddles are made of simpler materials such as coconut shells.

PIPA ("pi-pah")   A lute with four strings. It is held upright and its strings can be strummed or plucked. The pipa is a popular instrument in the towns along the Yangtze River. Entertainers in tea houses strum their instruments while telling stories or singing.

GUZHENG ("ku-zhehng") A large zither with 18 or 21 strings. It is played like a horizontal harp and sounds almost like one. In ancient times, playing the *guzheng* was considered a status symbol—to be able to play it was to be cultured.

ARCHITECTURE

Chinese buildings have distinctive roofs and structures constructed from a series of vertical wooden pillars that increase gradually in height, thus giving the roof its unique shape.

Chinese buildings are built in clusters. Courtyard-style houses have buildings on each side of a square with interconnecting halls. The main house faces south so that it is warm in winter and cool in summer. In the old days, the head of the household lived here, while the servants and children lived in the side buildings.

Temples and palaces have a similar layout. They are more elaborately built with more courtyards lying side by side or one behind the other.

One of the most charming aspects of Chinese buildings is their elaborate ornamentation. Beams are often of red lacquer with flowers painted on them. Figures of animals and people are painted on glazed tiles. Palaces are even more splendidly decorated with paintings of dragons and auspicious flowers and plants decorating ceilings, pillars, and walls. Doors of palaces are always painted red for good luck and have rows of nine gold studs running vertically and horizontally.

The Chinese believe that nine is the best number as it means a person is still in existence and still achieving. To reach 10 is to be at the end of the line.

Red lacquered pillars and decorated beams of a covered walkway built in the traditional style.

PAPER CUTOUTS

Women in the countryside may spend their free time cutting paper patterns. The patterns can be symmetrical or complicated, with birds, animals, flowers, or popular opera characters. Some can even be of an entire scene from daily life.

Paper cutouts are often used to decorate the house during festive seasons such as the Spring Festival. Usually stuck on lanterns, windows, doors, and walls, paper cutouts often are designs of flowers or symbols of good luck, longevity, and health. Paper cutouts of the double happiness character are used during weddings to adorn gifts and sacrificial offerings, on wedding dowries, candlesticks, and incense burners. Paper cutouts are also used as stencils for embroidery or indigo prints that go on clothes, bed linen, or curtains.

Papercutting designs are often handed down from generation to generation and differ from village to village. The appeal of this art form lies in its simplicity. It can be picked up and put down at any time.

The excitement of unfolding a paper cutout lies in the fact that one never knows what to expect from a piece. Each piece is an original in itself.

EMBROIDERY

Embroidery was refined to an art form by women who wanted to wear something more than plain cloth. In the old days, a girl's embroidery skill would indicate whether she would make a good wife.

Embroidery was first used with the discovery of silk thread. Clothes, shoes, fans, purses, and hair accessories were decorated with embroidery. Motifs are different for men and women. Flowers, butterflies, geometric

Paper cutouts of an opera figure (*top*) and a historical event (*above*). Children and old folk are placed at the city gate to confuse attacking enemies.

designs, and phoenixes decorate women's clothes and accessories, while dragons and bold solid designs are considered masculine.

Embroidery is also used to decorate altar cloths, flags, banners, and wall hangings. The designs are often of calligraphic characters, scenes of nature, or images of people and animals.

Elaborate pieces of embroidery can take years to complete and are often worked on by more than one person. Suzhou, Hunan, Sichuan, and Guangdong are the embroidery centers of China. These regions have their own designs and styles. One of the most famous is the double-sided embroidery where the same image or sometimes a different one appears on the reverse side. The stitches of some pieces of embroidery are so fine that it is hard to tell one stitch from the next, and they look like paintings.

An embroidery of a landscape done in the style of a landscape painting.

99

LEISURE

MANY RECREATIONAL ACTIVITIES IN CHINA are concentrated around relaxing in the park, taking part in martial arts and sports, or playing games.

FUN IN THE PARK

Parks in urban China are seldom empty. As early as 5 A.M., the parks fill up with people. Most are the elderly who start their day with a session of *taijiquan* ("tie-chi-chuan") or *qigong* ("chi-kong"), both martial art forms, usually done en masse. People will join whoever is in motion; sometimes half the park is filled with strangers united in exercise. In the summer months some people may switch to aerobics.

Parks are also filled with bird song. The most popular is the Chinese thrush. Birds are kept in round, beautifully carved cages. Their cages are hung from the branches of trees, and the birds sing in competition with one another. Many Chinese keep birds as pets, although in the cities there are more pet cats and dogs. Dogs need a government license.

On Sundays groups of opera lovers and musicians gather in the parks to give impromptu performances. A person could start playing a fiddle while a passerby bursts into song, followed by another. When everything is over, they go their separate ways and may never perform together again.

On Sundays, families go to the park for a walk. The Chinese love posing for and taking photographs. They often pose with flowers, plants, statues, or anything that might make a good picture, sometimes waiting in line for a photograph of a commemorative statue or display.

Above: **A hobby with many Chinese is keeping songbirds that compete with other birds.**

Opposite: **An old man relaxes by playing the *erhu*, which is like a fiddle with two strings.**

Right: **Parents and children in the park.**

Below: **Tujia girls playing with stilts. Each girl is trying to force the other off her stilts.**

CHILDREN'S GAMES

Children in China play most of the same games as children around the world. Hopscotch, jump rope, marbles, and cat's cradle are all popular schoolyard games, while computer games are also catching on.

Boys also play a game with a heavy-based shuttlecock. They stand in a circle kicking the shuttlecock around trying to keep it up. In another game, a boy stands in the middle of a circle, tosses the ball high into the air, and shouts the name of a friend. The named person must catch the ball, go into the circle, and repeat the process. The person who fails to catch the ball or come to the center when his name is called is hit with the ball. This can be a painful game, but it is lots of fun.

Girls play with a thick rope made of rubber bands. It is stretched between two girls, while the rest take turns jumping in and out, twisting

THE STORYTELLER

Chinese storytellers perform to audiences of all ages. They entertain with epics, classics, martial arts stories, and contemporary stories. The props, if any, are simple— a fan or a table and chair. The storyteller makes a wide sweep with the fan and tells of soldiers thundering across the desert. The fan may also be a coy lady's accessory, or it could be slapped against the body to show the tyranny of an emperor. The table, likewise, could become the front of a bus, a magistrate's table, a counter in a department store, or a hospital bed.

The magic lies in the storytellers' skill. They change not only the tone of their voice to assume a different character, but their expressions and behavior as well. The beauty of it all is the audience never mixes up the characters or train of events.

This profession started out with itinerant storytellers who moved from village to village providing entertainment. Some would light a joss stick and time the story so that the most exciting part ended when the joss stick finished. A hat was passed around and the story would continue. Audiences laughed, cried, and trembled in fear with the storyteller.

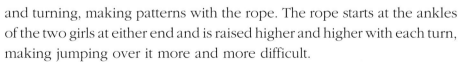

Many variety shows on stage and on television now include a storyteller. Another form of entertainment has evolved from this. Called crosstalk, it involves two or more performers playing out a comic script like standup comics of the West.

and turning, making patterns with the rope. The rope starts at the ankles of the two girls at either end and is raised higher and higher with each turn, making jumping over it more and more difficult.

Children in the countryside play simple games with whatever they can find. There is a game they play with pieces of paper the size of playing cards. If paper is not available, they use leaves. Each person has his or her share with one piece put in the center. The children then take turns trying to flip over the paper or leaf by slapping their own paper or leaf down near it. If the air current they produce succeeds in doing that, they get to keep the paper or leaf in the center.

An old man practicing *qigong*, a martial art that promotes health.

MARTIAL ARTS

Taijiquan and *qigong* are usually performed in the early morning. This is believed to be the best time, as *qi* ("chee"), "energy" or "force," can be drawn into the body to invigorate one's own *qi*.

TAIJIQUAN Used by the Chinese since the 17th century, *taijiquan* is made up of hundreds of different positions originally used in self-defense. It is also known as "shadow boxing," for smooth, graceful, circular movements are combined with deep breathing and performed with concentration. Perhaps the most beneficial feeling is the calmness that comes after the exercises.

Taijiquan has its origins in the preparation for combat. Controlled breathing and slow, circular body movements ensure that all the limbs and internal organs are exercised.

Taijiquan had only eight primary hand gestures and five body movements when it was first invented. More movements were added through the years and now there are five major styles of *taijiquan*. More recently developed styles include quick movements with lively footwork and movements borrowed from fencing.

QIGONG This is a deep-breathing exercise that regulates the mind and body. The aim of *qigong* is to achieve longevity. With breath control and concentration, *qi* can be directed to various parts of the body to increase strength and decrease pain. Some people use this skill to perform feats like lying under the wheels of a moving car or bending iron bars.

Qigong is used more as a therapeutic form of physical exercise than for amazing acts. It has been proven useful in controlling high blood pressure, heart disease, aches and pains, and breathing disorders. Therapeutic *qigong* can be done lying down, sitting, standing, or walking. It stresses the calming of the mind, concentration and regulating breathing. A combination of these stimulates the nervous system, increases blood circulation and metabolism, and puts the body on the road to self-renewal.

A *wushu* master giving a demonstration. *Wushu*, popularly known in the West as *kung fu*, is an art of self-defense rather than of attack.

WUSHU This art of fighting is thousands of years old. The four main categories of *wushu* ("woo-shoo") are: Chinese boxing with bare hands, duet boxing, sword play, and group exercise.

The most popular form of *wushu* is Chinese boxing, seen in *kung fu* movies where hands and legs move lightning fast, with long, high jumps. Of the many different forms of Chinese boxing, one is based on strength, while another requires cunning. The latter imitates the movements of 12 different birds and animals such as the dragon, tiger, monkey, horse, snake, eagle, sparrow, turtle, and even the praying mantis. Yet another form of Chinese boxing imitates drunkenness like the Eight Drunken Immortals or the Drunken Monkey.

Weapons used in *wushu* include the saber, spear, sword, clubs, and the nine-link chain. Students of *wushu* perform it for the beauty and exercise of the art rather than for fighting.

SPORTS

All forms of sports are popular in China. Schools, factories, and large organizations often have sporting facilities like basketball courts, Ping-Pong tables, and badminton nets and rackets. Some organizations reserve 10 or 20 minutes a day for mass exercises.

An improvised ping-pong table.

Ping-Pong, basketball, and volleyball are favorite sports. It is no wonder that the Chinese excel in them and produce some of the best international players.

Ping-Pong played an important part in restoring diplomatic relations between China and the United States. In a move known later as "Ping-Pong diplomacy," China invited a United States Ping-Pong team to China in 1971 and mended a 20-year rift.

The Chinese play Ping-Pong anywhere, both indoors and outdoors, on any surface on which a ping-pong ball can bounce.

In warmer weather, many Chinese swim in rivers and canals, disregarding "no swimming" signs. In winter, northerners use the same rivers and canals for ice skating.

Among China's minorities, sporting activities include Mongolian-style wrestling and horsemanship, Tibetan yak races, Korean spring board and swing, and the Miao's crossbow event.

BOARD GAMES

In a city park or quiet village square in the evening, men seated on low stools concentrate over a chessboard. They are playing elephant chess or *weiqi*, both strategy board games.

Elephant chess (*above*) has been around since A.D. 700. Chess pieces include cannons, elephants, cavalry, infantry, and chariots, with a fortress in which the king and his counselors are entrenched. The two halves of the chessboard are separated by the Yellow River. The objective is to storm the enemy's fortress and capture the king, who never leaves the fortress. Chessmen travel along lines, like in *weiqi*.

Weiqi ("way-chee"), or "go," is the oldest board game in China, having been around for thousands of years. *Wei* means "to surround" while *qi* means "board game." It is played with a grid board marked with 19 vertical and 19 horizontal lines and 181 black and 180 white flat, round counters. Players mark out their own territories and then try and capture each other's men and territory. Single or whole groups of men can be captured and removed from the board. The winner is the one who has gained the most territory and men.

Weiqi is considered the most complicated board game in the world because of the high number of possible moves.

FESTIVALS

THE CHINESE CALENDAR is basically an agricultural one that charts changes in season, temperature, rainfall, and growing cycle. It follows the passage of the moon and divides the year into 12 lunar months. This does not coincide with the Gregorian calendar followed by Western countries. Although the Western calendar has been adopted for daily use, some of the older generation use the Chinese calendar more than the Western one because it marks the seasons more accurately.

THE CHINESE ZODIAC

Legend has it that on his deathbed, the Buddha summoned all the animals of the kingdom to his bedside. Only 12 turned up, so in order of their appearance, he dedicated a year to each of them.

The Chinese zodiac moves in a cycle of 12 years and people born under these signs are said to possess certain characteristics.

Rat	1984, 1996, 2008, 2020	Charming, bright, creative, and thrifty
Ox	1985, 1997, 2009, 2021	Steadfast, methodical, and dependable
Tiger	1986, 1998, 2010, 2022	Dynamic, warm, sincere, and a leader
Rabbit	1987, 1999, 2011, 2023	Humble, artistic, and clearsighted
Dragon	1988, 2000, 2012, 2024	Flamboyant, imaginative, and lucky
Snake	1989, 2001, 2013, 2025	Discreet, sensual, refined, and intelligent
Horse	1990, 2002, 2014, 2026	Sociable, competitive, and stubborn
Sheep	1991, 2003, 2015, 2027	Artistic, fastidious, and indecisive
Monkey	1992, 2004, 2016, 2028	Witty, popular, versatile, and good-humored
Rooster	1993, 2005, 2017, 2029	Aggressive, alert, and a perfectionist
Dog	1994, 2006, 2018, 2030	Honest, conservative, and sympathetic
Pig	1995, 2007, 2019, 2031	Caring, industrious, and home-loving

Opposite: **Playing a game of riddles with lanterns during the Lantern Festival, celebrated on the 15th and last day of the Lunar New Year.**

MAJOR FESTIVALS

Lion dances accompanied by cymbals, drums, and gongs are a common sight during the Lunar New Year festivities. Celebrations for the Lunar New Year last for two weeks, although most people are back at work by the fourth day. On the 15th day, a lantern festival marks the end of the celebrations.

LUNAR NEW YEAR Falling on the first day of the first lunar month, this is the most important festival for Chinese in China and all around the world. It is usually between late January and late February and marks the beginning of spring, so it is also known as the Spring Festival.

Preparations start with spring cleaning and decorating the home with symbols of good luck. New clothes are bought, rice bins are filled to the brim, larders are stocked, quarrels are mended, and debts are paid.

The most important event of the New Year preparations is the reunion dinner. Children, no matter how far from home, make special efforts to be home with their parents on New Year's Eve. Certain foods are a must on the table. For example, in the north, *jiao zi* ("chi-ao zher"), or dumplings, are shaped like gold ingots to represent wealth.

At midnight on New Year's Eve, firecrackers are set off to scare away any evil spirits. All lights in the house are turned on to chase away bad luck.

On the first day of the New Year, people dress in new clothes to visit relatives. Children kneel and pay their respects to their elders. In return, they receive little red packets with money inside. Nothing unpleasant is allowed to happen on this day to ensure good fortune for the rest of the year.

QINGMING JIE ("ching-ming ji-eh") The "clear and bright festival" comes around in early spring. On this day the Chinese remember their dead ancestors, visiting cemeteries to sweep the ancestors' tombs clean and to pay respects to them. This is not a solemn day as one would imagine. Burial grounds are usually in the countryside so visits to the cemetery are turned into family outings. Picnics and activities such as kite-flying make these visits a festive affair.

ZHONGQIU JIE ("chong-chi-you ji-eh") The 15th day of the eighth lunar month marks the time when the moon is at its fullest and brightest. This is when the Chinese celebrate the Mid-Autumn Festival. The autumn weather is at its best, and people come out at night to admire the moon and enjoy the weather.

Mooncakes made of a thin pastry filled with sweet mashed lotus seeds are eaten and given as gifts. The night is also filled with lights from paper lanterns. Children are often busy looking for the lady in the moon, having often heard the legend about how she got there.

The legend says that a lady, Chang Er, had a husband who was a tyrannical king. He had a potion that could make him immortal. Fearing for her people, Chang Er stole the potion and drank it. She became immortal and immediately flew to the moon where she has been ever since.

Chinese who are Taoist-Buddhist have altars and incense burners at home, for either ancestors or deities or both. On the first and 15th day of every lunar month, they burn joss sticks for their ancestors and deities. The more devout keep a vegetarian diet on these days.

During the Nu Torch Festival men and women dressed in traditional costumes, gather for torch games and song and dance. The Yi have a similar torch festival during which men and women look for potential spouses.

DUANWU JIE ("tu-ahn-wu ji-eh") This festival is held on the fifth day of the fifth lunar month and is known as the Dragon Boat Festival. It is held to remember a patriotic poet who drowned himself because his state was taken over by a neighboring state. Villagers rushed to the river and threw in rice dumplings to prevent the fish from eating his body. They spent days in a boat trying to recover his body; all they had to eat were rice dumplings filled with meat and wrapped in bamboo leaves. To remember this day, dragon boat races are held and rice dumplings are eaten.

MINORITY FESTIVALS

TIBETAN BATHING FESTIVAL Between late summer and early autumn when the Wild Rat star is sighted in Lhasa, Tibetans celebrate the Bathing Festival. The festival lasts for seven days until the star is out of sight.

Legend has it that during an epidemic, the Goddess of Mercy, Guan Yin, sent down seven fairies with seven bottles of holy water to be put into the rivers, lakes, and ponds of Tibet. That night, everyone in Tibet dreamed that a girl covered in sores bathed in a river and was immediately cured. The next morning, all the sick people rushed to bathe in the rivers and were cured. Tibetans now celebrate the festival by bathing and washing their clothes in rivers. While the clothes and linens line the banks of rivers to dry, their owners indulge their festive mood by drinking copious amounts of barley wine and buttered tea.

DAI WATER SPLASHING FESTIVAL The Dai minority of Yunnan celebrate the second day of their New Year by splashing water on each other. This is done to shower blessings and to wish for happiness. The more water, the more wishes. This means buckets of fun. The elderly are the only ones spared from this. Ladles of water are poured down their backs or drops of water from wet olive branches are spinkled on their heads while good wishes are uttered.

PUBLIC HOLIDAYS

China has fewer public holidays than most other countries in the world. But these include three one-week holiday periods for the Spring Festival, Labor Day (May 1), and National Day (October 1). These longer holidays are intended to encourage citizens to travel and spend more to help economic growth. Only New Year's Day (January 1) remains a one-day holiday.

National Day is one of the grandest public celebrations in China. Beijing celebrates with elaborate fireworks and mass formation dances at Tiananmen Square.

If a public holiday falls early in the week, like on Tuesday, the Chinese prefer to work on Sunday and take Monday and Tuesday off.

Some holidays are only for certain groups of people. On March 8, International Working Women's Day, Chinese women get half a day off from work. International Children's Day on June 1 means no school. May 4 is Chinese Youth Day when older children get half a day off from school.

The National Day Parade at Changan Avenue in Beijing is a spectacular sight as columns of men and women representing various organizations march in procession.

FOOD

A DAILY ACTIVITY that the Chinese most enjoy is eating. *"Chi le ma?"* ("cheh leh mah"), meaning "have you eaten yet?" often follows *"Ni hao"* ("ni how"), meaning "hello," or "how are you." Sometimes people do not even say hello, but ask whether you have had a meal.

Because of poverty, the Chinese have developed unique styles of cooking. Stir frying food cut up into small, even pieces that cook quickly saves precious firewood, as does braising and simmering soups on the same fire used to warm the house. To make full use of an animal that is killed for food, the Chinese have invented a recipe for every part of the animal, except the fur or feathers.

KITCHEN ESSENTIALS

The Chinese cook their food on burners, fueled by firewood in the country and gas in the city. The kitchen may have a few fancy appliances, the most popular being the electric rice cooker. The most important utensils are the cleaver, wok, a soup ladle, and a pair of chopsticks.

The Chinese cleaver is a heavy knife with a broad, rectangular blade. Kept razor-sharp, it can hack hard bones and slice and shred meat and vegetables very finely. The flat side of the cleaver is used to bruise ginger and garlic, while the blunt edge tenderizes meat and knocks out live fish. The end of the handle is used to crush garlic and mash black beans.

The wok is an all-purpose cooking utensil. It is best made of cast iron, but it is common to find woks in stainless steel, aluminium, or a nonstick material. The wok is a half sphere with two handles on opposite sides. It is used for deep frying, shallow frying, stir frying, boiling, and simmering. Sometimes a pair of chopsticks is placed across the bottom over water, and a bowl is balanced on the chopsticks to steam food inside the bowl.

Below: **Every kitchen has the versatile wok, used to steam, fry, boil, braise, and simmer food. It usually comes with a dome-shaped cover to trap the steam and cook food more quickly.**

Opposite: **The wedding feast, ready to go to the groom's home, is part of the bride's dowry.**

RICE

Rice is so important to the Chinese that *fan* ("fun"), meaning rice, refers to a whole meal (*above*). Many Chinese sayings revolve around rice. The breadwinner is one who "puts rice on the table," while to "break someone's rice bowl" means to make another lose his or her job. If a Chinese asks you to come and eat rice, he or she is inviting you to a meal.

Rice is treated with utmost respect. Every spilled grain is picked up, washed, and cooked. Parents persuade their children to eat up every grain of rice in their bowl by telling them that a bowl dotted with rice grains means that they will marry someone with pockmarked skin. *Fan* is eaten with *cai* ("chai"), a general term for dishes that accompany rice.

An unusual rice recipe is exploded rice. Uncooked rice is put into a drum that is heated over charcoal to a high temperature. It is rotated and when the meter reaches a certain pressure a valve is released, and with a bang, the rice grains spill out into a waiting bag. The grains look and taste like Rice Krispies and are eaten as a snack or pressed together with sweet syrup to make a cookie.

CHOPSTICKS

Chinese started eating with chopsticks 3,000 years ago. They were probably invented to pick up bite-sized pieces of food. Soldiers going to war had a special kit consisting of a cutting knife and a pair of chopsticks. Regular chopsticks are tapered, slim objects with a blunt end. They are about 8 inches (20.3 cm) long, though those used for cooking may be 2 feet (0.6 m) long.

Chopsticks are usually made of wood, bamboo, or plastic. The more elaborate ones have cloisonné designs or are made of ivory or jade. Emperors ate with silver chopsticks that they believed would turn black if the food was poisoned.

Chinese use chopsticks to eat everything except soup. They use chopsticks to push rice from the bowl into the mouth, to pick up portions of food, and even to eat cake! Children start using chopsticks as soon as they can hold a pair and coordinate their movements. There is no rule as to how they should be used, except that they should never cross.

REGIONAL CUISINE

BEIJING CUISINE   This northern cuisine is characterized by the liberal use of garlic and chilies. Food is often drenched in oil and seasoned with vinegar, salt, and sugar. Less rice is eaten in the north as wheat grows better in the drier weather. Plain steamed buns or wheat pancakes are eaten as a staple, with stir-fried dishes of diced meat and vegetables or stewed meats. Wheat dumplings stuffed with minced meat and vegetables are eaten as a main meal especially in winter.

Beijing food also includes dishes from neighboring Mongolia. One of the most popular is skewered mutton. Sold along the streets, skewered mutton is fried in oil and rolled in powdered chili and cumin. Mongolian rinsed mutton is also popular. Diners sit around a charcoal-heated funneled pot, dipping thin slices of mutton into the hot water. The barely cooked meat is dipped into a fermented bean curd sauce and eaten with Chinese cabbage and thin noodles.

Fish farming in Wuxi. Fish breeding has been practiced in China for centuries. China's long coastline provides large regions with abundant fish, while rivers and lakes supply freshwater fish to landlocked provinces.

SHANGHAI CUISINE This covers the lower Yangtze river delta. This region is known as the Land of Rice and Fish, and its cuisine revolves around whatever can be caught in the rivers. Fish, eels, and shrimps are steamed or cooked in tasty soy- and sugar-based sauces. Another favorite condiment is black vinegar, which is used as a dip or in a sauce. As in northern cuisine, a lot of oil and chilies are used, and the simple cooking methods bring out the best flavor of the food.

SICHUAN CUISINE Sichuan has the spiciest food in China. Most dishes are covered in a red chili oil and sprinkled with a potent, fragrant pepper. This pepper has a delayed numbing effect on the tongue that can deaden all sense of taste for several seconds.

As fish is hard to come by in Sichuan, pork, beef, and eggplant are more usually cooked in a fish-flavoured sauce. This is actually a mixture of vinegar, hot bean paste, ginger, garlic, and scallions.

Other Sichuan specialties include camphor- and tea-smoked duck, where the bird is slowly smoked over a fire of camphor chips and tea leaves. The fragrant duck is then deep-fried and eaten with a thick, sweet soy sauce. *Dan dan* ("dahn dahn") noodles are also a favorite. Cold boiled noodles are tossed into a bowl and seasoned with chili oil, ginger juice, garlic paste, soy sauce, vinegar, and sugar. Sometimes, this is topped with shreds of cucumber and sesame seed paste.

A restaurant window in the town of Guanxian, Sichuan. Note the string of green chilies in the center. Sichuan food is well-known for its spiciness.

CANTONESE CUISINE Ths is the best known form of Chinese cuisine outside China. The Cantonese are known to be very fussy about the freshness of the ingredients in their dishes. Dishes are never overcooked, and flavors are seldom masked with heavy, spicy, or pungent sauces. Vegetables are lightly stir-fried or blanched in hot water and dressed with oyster sauce.

The Cantonese are also famous for their thin egg noodles, which are eaten with a dumpling soup or topped with red-roasted meats. Soups are an integral part of Cantonese cuisine. Sometimes boiled with traditional Chinese herbs, these soups are simmered for hours over a charcoal fire and the rich, tasty soup is drunk as part of dinner.

CHINESE EXOTICA

"If it moves and its back faces the sun, the Chinese will eat it." The Cantonese are especially famous for their exotic taste in meat. Snake meat is made into a thick soup, while dog meat is roasted or stewed. Hard-to-find iguanas are suspended in wine and eaten in small amounts for their tonic effect. The Chinese believe that the more exotic the meat is, the better its effects on one's health. Dried pieces of crocodile meat made into a soup, for example, are said to do wonders for a child's cough.

Bear paws are hard to find, but when they are available they are braised and served to very important guests. Braised camel hooves, another delicacy, have a gelatinous texture and no particular taste. Fortunately or unfortunately, the Chinese camel has two humps. Braised in stock, they look and taste like lumps of fat. Camels' noses are not spared either. Since each camel has only one nose, they are a much rarer delicacy.

Other Chinese delicacies include bird's nests, that is, the dried mucus from a swallow's salivary glands that the bird uses to line its home. Served in sweet or savory

Frogs' legs fried in ginger and scallions are said to strengthen one's legs.

soups, bird's nests are regarded as a delicacy and a tonic. Shark's fins are made into a rich, thick soup, while sea slugs and jellyfish may be prepared in a variety of ways.

Century eggs start as fresh eggs covered in an alkaline ash and kept for a month or longer in a cool dark place. By then, the egg white has turned into a black jelly and the yellow yolk is ringed with grey. This is often eaten as an appetizer with vinegar or pickled ginger.

OODLES OF NOODLES

Noodles, or *mien* in Chinese, come in all shapes, sizes, and lengths. In the north, they are made of plain wheat and water and look like flat spaghetti. They can be eaten plain, dressed in garlic, chilies, and vinegar, boiled in a plain soup, or fried with chives and soy sauce.

In western China, *shou mien* ("show mi-an"), or hand noodles, and *la mien* ("lah mi-an"), pulled noodles, are more popular. Hand noodles are made with the same wheat-and-water dough, but bits of dough are plucked and thrown into boiling water. With pulled noodles, bits of dough are pulled into thick lengths before being boiled. Both these noodles are fried in a tomato-basd sauce with onions, bell peppers, and bits of mutton.

Noodles drying in the sun. There is a debate as to who invented noodles. The Chinese claim that Marco Polo took the art of noodle-making from China to Italy, while the Italians like to believe that he brought his skill of noodle-making with him to China.

In Shanxi province, cut noodles are a specialty. Lumps of dough are held in the hand and slices are cut off into a boiling pot of water. Master noodle-makers are so skilled that they balance lumps of dough on their hats while they slice off pieces with knives held in each hand.

In the south, eggs are added to the wheat dough. Sometimes a few drops of alkaline water are added to give the noodles a slightly bitter but pleasant taste. Rice flour is also used to make noodles in the south. Noodles here are round or flat and can be as thick as spaghetti or as fine as hair. They are fried soft or crispy, topped with a hearty sauce of shrimp and pork, or added to a rich soup.

Long noodles symbolize a long life and are served at birthday celebrations.

When Chinese eat out, the decor of the restaurant is often the least important factor. Most Chinese restaurants are simply furnished with bare essentials.

Banquet tables, complete with plates of snacks, ready for the guests.

BANQUETS

Chinese banquets are long, noisy meals that leave one absolutely stuffed with food. Snacks like peanuts, candied walnuts, or pickled cabbage are served before the meal starts. Sometimes cold cuts will be laid on the table before the guests arrive.

There are usually 10 guests at each round table. At each setting is a small

LETTUCE IN OYSTER SAUCE

This vegetable dish is quick and easy to whip up and tastes amazingly good. For the Chinese, no meal is complete without at least one green leafy vegetable dish.

1 ½ teaspoons vegetable oil
1 pot boiling water
½ head of lettuce leaves
2 tablespoons oyster sauce
2 teaspoons soy sauce
Pepper to taste

Put ½ teaspoon of vegetable oil in a pot of boiling water. Put lettuce leaves in boiling water for about 15 seconds, then remove and arrange on a plate. Mix remaining oil, oyster sauce, soy sauce, and pepper in a bowl. Pour this sauce over the lettuce leaves and serve.

saucer for soy sauce, a plate, a small bowl, a pair of chopsticks, a spoon, and some glasses for soft drinks and alcoholic beverages.

Dinner starts with hor d'oeuvres, which are a mixture of hot and cold dishes like seasoned jellyfish and century eggs. The platter is often elaborately decorated with the food making geometric designs or forming part of a peacock's tail. Guests usually help themselves and the host will always make sure that their plates are constantly full.

Dishes are served one at a time, to be admired before being consumed. There are usually 10 dishes at a banquet. The next-to-last dish is usually a soup to wash everything down, followed by fried rice or noodles to "fill the stomach" just in case one did not have enough.

Dessert at the end may be a flaky pastry filled with mashed beans or nuts, or a sweet soup of whole beans or nuts and a fruit platter.

The most elaborate of Chinese banquets is the emperor's banquet that consists of 132 courses, all at one sitting. No wonder the Chinese equivalent for *bon appetit* is *man man chi* ("mun-mun-cheh"), meaning "please eat slowly."

A large fresh-food market in Beijing. The produce of the region determines type of food cooked and the cuisine.

HOMECOOKED MEALS

Chinese are particular about the freshness of their food, so shopping for fresh ingredients, especially vegetables, is a daily affair. They buy whatever foods are in season.

In the north, for example, meals in winter use Chinese cabbage. This hardy vegetable is grown in autumn and survives the bitterly cold winter. Outer leaves are removed to reveal fresh, crispy leaves within.

Breakfast is usually a thin rice porridge made from leftover rice or broken rice grains too small to make a good pot of rice. It is eaten with a wide variety of pickled vegetables or pieces of salty fermented bean curd. In the south, meat and eggs are added to the porridge to make a tasty dish called congee. Fried dough sticks, unleavened bread sprinkled with sesame seeds, or noodles are sometimes eaten.

Dinner is the main meal of the day and is eaten early, between 5 and 6 P.M. Family members sit around a table filled with dishes. The soup is usually in the middle, surrounded by two or three dishes of vegetables and a main dish of fish, poultry, or pork. Family members have a bowl of rice each and help themselves from the common dishes.

Chinese cooking is a balance of contrasting tastes and textures. There will never be two sweet-sour dishes or two deep-fried dishes on the same table. Soups are served as part of a meal and are used to cleanse and refresh the palate during the meal.

TABLE MANNERS

Do not be surprised if a Chinese eats noisily at the table. It is not considered bad manners to slurp soup, although it is poor upbringing if one chews noisily. Using chopsticks as drumsticks on the table is disrespectful. Chopsticks are also never used to point at a person or gesticulate with during a conversation.

A meal only starts when everyone is seated. Children invite their elders to eat before starting their own meals. Usually, a mouthful of plain rice is eaten first before any of the other dishes are touched. A person first helps himself or herself to the nearest dish. Food taken from any dish must be from the part of the plate nearest the

Sitting down to a meal together.

person. Morsels of food must be taken from the top. It is rude to flip over pieces of food or take pieces from the bottom of the plate. A person also never chooses the best pieces, which are offered to the oldest person at the table or the guest.

Chinese think it is perfectly all right to put the bones on the table. In some local restaurants, bones are even deposited on the floor.

Chicken is not chicken on a Chinese menu, but rather the more fanciful "phoenix."

WHAT'S IN A NAME?

Chinese get very poetic about the names of their dishes. Reading a menu is sometimes like reading a fairy tale; no food is mentioned, only phoenixes, jade stalks, and lions' heads. Spinach served with boiled bean curd is known as Red-Beaked Green Parrots on White Marble, while a Lion's Head is a meatball the size of a baseball.

Ants Crawling Up A Tree Trunk is less dangerous than one may think. It is only ground meat cooked with transparent bean noodles. Pockmarked Bean Curd sounds unappetizing, but is named after a woman with unfortunate skin who invented the dish of bean curd cooked with minced meat and hot broad-bean paste. This dish, with white pieces of bean curd swimming in a sauce red with chili oil and bits of minced pork, does look like a skin problem.

Red-Cooked Water Paddles are quite tasty, consisting of fish fins cooked in a soybean sauce. Drunken Chicken is cold chicken marinated in wine. Beggar's Chicken has a more colorful background. A beggar once stole a chicken and, afraid of being discovered, coated it with mud, feathers and all, and threw it into a fire. When the coast was clear, he cracked open the hardened mud and found that the chicken was fragrant and delicious.

Monk Jumps Over The Wall is one of the most expensive dishes one can order. It consists of all sorts of dried seafood stewed slowly in a clay pot. The story goes that a meditating monk was distracted by a wonderful aroma wafting over a wall. After a while, he could not stand it any longer and jumped over the wall to ask for a taste.

WINE

Chinese wines are made from rice, sorghum, millet, or grapes that are naturally fermented. The most popular wines are made from rice. The three main types of wine are white wine, yellow wine, and burning wine, which is high in alcohol.

White wine is made from glutinous rice and is light and sweet. Yellow wine is also made from rice and has a stronger flavor, turning darker with age. Chinese spirits are potent, often colorless liquids that can make one's mouth and stomach seem on fire. The Chinese like to drink their wine warm and in small cups, which they empty in one gulp.

There are many stories about Chinese wine. One of the most famous Chinese poets, Li Bai, is said to have written his best pieces while intoxicated. Many of his poems speak of the joys of wine and the wonderful companion it makes. He is believed to have drowned while trying to rescue the moon. In his drunken state, he thought it had fallen in the lake.

Another tale tells of an emperor's forgotten pot of rice that fermented into wine. It tasted so good that there was a tasting party that left everyone with a hangover. The emperor then decreed that wine should always be drunk from tiny cups, that it must always be taken with food, and that mild mental or physical exercise should be done when drinking wine.

In Shaoxing, famous for its yellow wine, a father seals and buries an earthen jar of good wine the day his daughter is born. This wine is unearthed when the girl marries and is used as part of her wedding celebrations.

Wine fermenting in a cellar. One of the most famous Chinese wines is Maotai, a transparent, potent spirit made from sorghum.

A teahouse in Sichuan. Drinking tea has been popular among the Chinese for thousands of years, as revealed by literary references as early as A.D. 270. It is said that a few leaves of the camellia tree accidentally fell into an ancient sage's pot of boiling water. He found the brew pleasant and repeated the experiment. Thus, tea was born.

TEA

Tea is the most important beverage in China. It is drunk at all times of the day insead of water. In ancient China it was used for medicinal purposes, and modern Chinese still swear by it. They believe it stimulates the digestive and nervous sysems and the heart, reduces the harmful effects of smoking and alcohol, and reduces fat.

Most of China's tea grows in the south. The finest teas are found growing on mist-covered cliffs so high up that trained monkeys are used to pluck them.

There are three types of tea: green, red, and oolong ("black dragon"). Green tea is a light refreshing drink made from dried young tea leaves. Red tea is made from leaves that have been fermented and toasted, making a stronger, more flavorful tea. Oolong tea is made from partially fermented leaves and is the most widely drunk tea in China and abroad. Sometimes jasmine flowers are added in the fermentation process of green or oolong tea to perfume it.

FACTS ABOUT TEA

- On formal occasions, tea (*right*) is served in a covered teacup that sits on a saucer. Leaves are left in the cup and the tea is drunk with the cover on to strain the tea leaves.
- When one's cup is refilled with water, it is polite to rap one's knuckles on the table three times to indicate thanks. This gesture was started by court officials who accompanied a Qing emperor traveling incognito. When he refilled their tea cups, they rapped thrice, representing the kowtows of thanks they could not perform.
- There are 30 types of tea in the world. All of them are found growing in Yunnan province.
- Frugal Chinese never throw away their used tea leaves. Some leave them on a saucer in a cupboard to absorb unpleasant smells. Others dry them in the sun and use them to make light and cool pillows.
- Tea is also used in the kitchen to smoke meat or boiled with soy sauce and eggs to make delicately flavored "tea eggs."
- Chinese porcelain was shipped to the West in wooden crates filled with tea as a shock

absorber. Both were sold at exorbitant prices.
- The Chinese drink their tea without milk or sugar. Tea is considered yin, or cooling, and the old Chinese will shake their heads at the idea of drinking iced tea.
- A marriage is recognized when tea served by the bride is formally accepted by the bride's parents-in-law.
- Garlic breath from a Chinese meal can be eliminated by chewing the tea leaves from one's cup. The chlorophyll in the leaves will freshen breath.

Everyday tea is made by adding hot water to a spoonful of tea leaves; with additions of water they last the whole day. The water should just come to a boil, then be poured into a warmed teapot holding the tea leaves. The tea is allowed to stand for three to five minutes and drunk from porcelain cups. Tea connoisseurs make their tea in tiny brown clay teapots that hold about a tablespoon of tea leaves. Hot water is added to the leaves and thrown away. The second addition of hot water brings out the flavor of the tea.

PEKING DUCK

Large pot of water
1 whole duck, giblets removed
1 teaspoon freshly ground white pepper
1 teaspoon sesame oil
2 teaspoons peanut oil
$^{1}/_{2}$ teaspoon ground star anise
$^{3}/_{4}$ cup red wine vinegar
1 $^{1}/_{2}$ tablespoons ground cinnamon
1 $^{1}/_{2}$ tablespoons ground ginger
$^{3}/_{4}$ cup brown sugar

Bring water to the boil. Remove from the stove and lower duck into the water. Leave for 5 minutes. Remove duck and pat dry.

Combine the other ingredients in a small saucepan and bring to the boil. Turn off the heat and leave the mixture to cool to room temperature.

Liberally coat the duck with the mixture and leave to sit at room temperature for 3 hours so that the coating dries out. Place duck on a rack, breast side up, in a preheated 350°F (177°C) oven for 2 to 2 $^{1}/_{2}$ hours. Roast until skin is crisp and brown.

Check occasionally and regulate the temperature so that the coating does not burn. Leave duck to cool to room temperature. Carefully carve pieces from the bone, being sure to include some of the crisp skin with each piece.

BRAISED CHICKEN

1 whole chicken
2 scallion stalks
2 or 3 slices fresh ginger root
4 tablespoons oil
3 tablespoons sherry
1/2 cup oyster sauce

2 cups water
1/2 teaspoon salt
6 dried black mushrooms, soaked in water
6 Chinese red dates*
1 tablespoon sugar
1 Chinese parsley

With a cleaver, chop chicken in 1 1/2 to 2-inch (3.8 to 5.1-cm) sections. Trim scallion stalks and slice ginger root. Heat oil in a large heavy pan and brown chicken sections quickly. Add sherry, oyster sauce, water, salt, scallions, and ginger root. Bring to a boil, then cover and simmer for 20 to 30 minutes. Add black mushrooms, red dates, and sugar. Simmer for 10 to 15 minutes. Transfer chicken sections to a serving bowl. Strain sauce and pour over chicken. Garnish with Chinese parsley and serve.

(*Chinese red dates and oyster sauce can be purchased in a grocery store specializing in Chinese foods.)

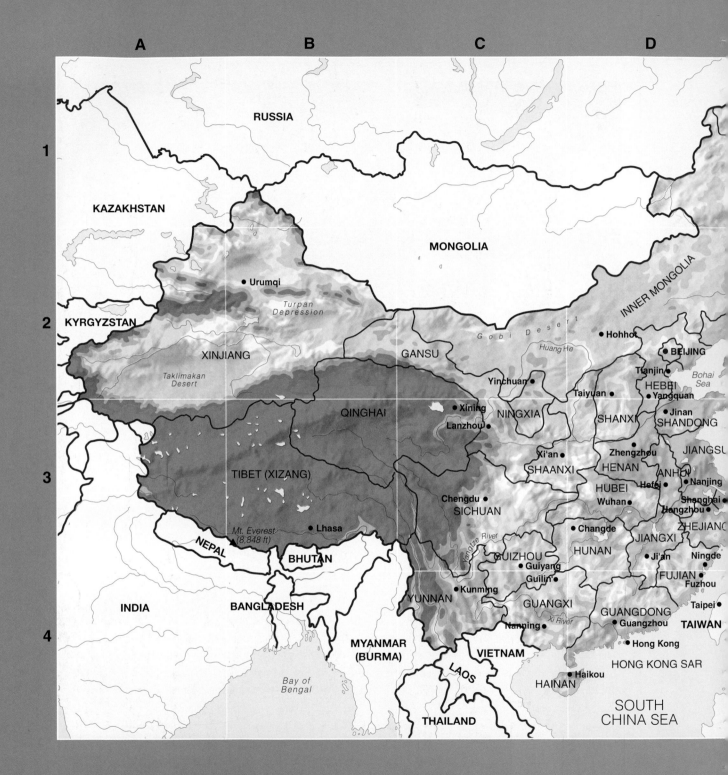

A B C D

1

KAZAKHSTAN

RUSSIA

MONGOLIA

INNER MONGOLIA

KYRGYZSTAN

2

• Urumqi

Turpan Depression

Gobi Desert

Huang He

• Hohhot

XINJIANG

GANSU

• BEIJING

Taklimakan Desert

Yinchuan •

• Xining

NINGXIA

Tianjin •

HEBEI

• Yangquan

Bohai Sea

Taiyuan •

QINGHAI

Lanzhou •

SHANXI

• Jinan

SHANDONG

Xi'an •

• Zhengzhou

JIANGSU

SHAANXI

HENAN

ANHUI

TIBET (XIZANG)

3

Chengdu •

HUBEI

Hefei •

• Nanjing

Wuhan •

Shanghai •

SICHUAN

Hangzhou •

ZHEJIANG

▲ Mt. Everest
(8,848 ft)

• Lhasa

Yangtze River

• Changde

HUNAN

JIANGXI

NEPAL

BHUTAN

GUIZHOU

• Guiyang

• Ji'an

Ningde •

INDIA

BANGLADESH

Guilin •

FUJIAN

• Fuzhou

YUNNAN

• Kunming

GUANGXI

Nanning •

Xi River

GUANGDONG

• Guangzhou

Taipei •

TAIWAN

MYANMAR
(BURMA)

VIETNAM

LAOS

• Hong Kong

HONG KONG SAR

Bay of Bengal

HAINAN

• Haikou

SOUTH
CHINA SEA

THAILAND

4

N

HEILONGJIANG

● Harbin

● Changchun
JILIN

● Shenyang
LIAONING

NORTH
KOREA

SEA OF
JAPAN

Yellow
Sea

SOUTH
KOREA

EAST
CHINA SEA

● Capital city
● Major town
▲ Mountain peak

Feet	Meters
16,500	5,000
9,900	3,000
6,600	2,000
3,300	1,000
1,650	500
660	200
0	0

MAP OF CHINA

Anhui, D3

Beijing, D2
Bangladesh, B4
Bay of Bengal, A4–C4
Bhutan, B3
Bohai Sea, D2

Changchun, E2
Changde, D3
Chengdu, C3

East China Sea, E3

Fujian, D3–D4
Fuzhou, D4

Gansu, B2, C2–C3
Gobi Desert, C2–D2
Guangdong, D4
Guangxi, C4
Guangzhou, D4
Guilin, C4
Guiyang, C3
Guizhou, C3–C4

Haikou, D4
Hainan, C4–D4
Hangzhou, D3
Harbin, E2
Hebei, D2–D3
Hefei, D3
Heilongjiang, D1, E1–E2
Henan, D3
Hohhot, D2
Hong Kong SAR, D4
Huang He, C2–C3, D2
Hubei, C3–D3
Hunan, C3, D3–D4

India, A3–A4, B4
Inner, Mongolia D2

Ji'an, D3
Jiangsu, D3
Jiangxi, D3–D4
Jilin, D2–E2
Jinan, D3

Kazakhstan, A1–A2, B1
Kunming, C4
Kyrgystan, A2

Lanzhou, C3
Laos, C4
Lhasa, B3
Liaoning, D2–E2

Mongolia, B1–B2, C1–
  C2, D1, D2
Mt Everest, B3
Myanmar (Burma),
  B3–B4, C3–C4

Nanjing, D3
Nanning, C4
Nepal, A3–B3
Ningde, D3
Ningxia, C2–C3
North Korea, E2

Qinghai, B2–B3, C2–C3

Russia, A1–D1

Shaanxi, C3, D2–D3
Shandong, D2–D3
Shanghai, D3
Shanxi, D2–D3
Shenyang, E2

Sichuan, C3
South China Sea, C4–D4
South Korea, E2–E3

Taipei, D4
Taiwan, D4
Taiyuan, D2
Taklimakan Desert, A2
Thailand, C4
Tianjin, D2
Turpan Depression, B2

Urumqi, B2

Vietnam, C4

Wuhan, D3

Xi River, C4–D4
Xi'an, C3
Xining, C3
Xinjiang, A2–A3, B1–B3
Xizang (Tibet), A3–C3

Yangquan, D2
Yangtze River, C3
Yellow Sea, D3–E3
Yinchuan, C2

Zhejiang, D3
Zhengzhou, D3

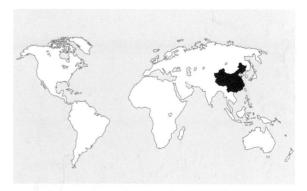

ECONOMIC CHINA

Agriculture

 Cotton

 Rice

 Tea

 Wheat

Manufacturing

 Aircraft

 Silk

 Steel

 Textiles

Vehicles

Natural Resources

 Copper

Coal

Gold

 Hydroelectricity

 Oil and Natural Gas

ABOUT
THE ECONOMY

OVERVIEW

China is a socialist market economy where some forms of capitalist market principles come into play. The government introduced reforms in the 1980s that ushered in two decades of phenomenal economic growth and helped modernize many parts of the country. China is one of the world's biggest recipients of foreign investment and aid. China has vast resources waiting to be tapped, and its industries, including agriculture, are being modernized to increase efficiency.

GROSS DOMESTIC PRODUCT (GDP)

US$1.08 trillion (2001)

GDP SECTORS

Agriculture: 17.7 percent (1999)
Industry: 49.3 percent (1999)
Service: 33 percent (1999)

WORKFORCE

711.5 million (2000)

UNEMPLOYMENT RATE

3.1 percent (2000)

CURRENCY

1 yuan (CNY) = 100 fen
Notes: 10, 20, 50 fen; 1, 2, 5, 10, 20, 50, 100 yuan
Coins: 1, 2, 10, 50 fen; 1 yuan
1 USD = 8.3 CNY (2001)
The yuan is called renmimbi (RMB) in China.

INFLATION RATE

0.4 percent (2000 estimate)

LAND USE

Arable land: 13.5 percent (1999)
Forests and woodland: 16.6 percent (1999)
Others: 26.4 percent (1999)

AGRICULTURAL PRODUCTS

Rice, wheat, cotton, meat, vegetables, poultry, dairy products, fish, oils, tea, flowers

MAJOR EXPORTS

Textiles, agricultural products, silk, tea, food products

MAJOR IMPORTS

Oil, agricultural products, aircraft, steel, semiconductors

MAJOR TRADING PARTNERS

United States, Japan, Hong Kong, Taiwan, European Union

HIGHWAYS

869,920 miles (1.4 million km) (1999)

RAILROADS

41,958 miles (67,524 km) (1999)

WATERWAYS

68,351 miles (110,000 km) (1999)

INTERNET ACCESS

Service Providers (ISPs): 3 (2000)
Users: 22 million (2001)

CULTURAL CHINA

Grand Buddha
The 233-foot (71-m) sculpture is the largest Buddha in the world, located at Leshan in Sichuan province. Construction began in A.D. 714, and was completed 90 years later.

Qinghai Lake (Koko Nor)
China's largest fish-rich lake is 10,500 feet (3,200 m) above sea level and 186 miles (300 km) west of Qinghai's capital city, Xining. The main attraction here is Bird Island, a breeding ground for wild geese, gulls, cormorants, sandpipers, and other species.

Forbidden City
The Forbidden City in Beijing, once off-limits to the common people, was home to emperors of the Ming and Qing dynasties. Construction was completed in 1420 after the Ming rulers moved the capital to Beijing. Also called the Palace Museum, the City was looted heavily during the Japanese invasion. The Kuomintang also removed valuable relics and treasures.

Great Wall
Construction of one of the Seven Wonders of the ancient world began in the 7th century B.C.when vassal states started building walls to fend off invading forces. With China unified under Qin rule in 221 B.C., segments of the wall were joined to keep out northern invaders.

Harbin
The capital city of Heilongjiang, the northernmost province of China. The city is famous for its Ice Lantern Festival in the winter, with fanciful sculptures of various shapes and forms of animals, people, and plants.

The Bund
Shanghai's lengthy waterfront overlooking the Huangpu River boasts colonial architecture that is reminiscent of the city's past as the greatest commercial city in the East. The bund is an Anglo-Indian term.

Potala Palace
Located in Lhasa, the Potala Palace was built between 1642 and 1650 for the fifth Dalai Lama. Later it was home to the Tibetan government. It was slightly damaged during Tibetan resistance to the Chinese invasion in 1959.

Jiuzhaigou National Park
A nature reserve in northern Sichuan with peaks, waterfalls, ponds, lakes, and forests. The area also has several Tibetan settlements.

Guilin
Guilin is China's world-famous picture-perfect city of mountains and lakes. The famed city was founded during the Qin Dynasty and developed as a transportation hub. During the 1930s and World War II, Guilin was a stronghold of the Communists.

Three Gorges
China's famous Three Gorges straddles two provinces—the Qutang and Wuxia gorges in Sichuan province and the Xiling gorge in Hubei province. Limestone cliffs tower on either side of China's longest river, the Yangtze. The scenic Three Gorges will be submerged as a result of the construction nearby of the world's largest dam, the Three Gorges Dam, expected to be completed by 2009.

ABOUT THE CULTURE

OFFICIAL NAME
People's Republic of China

CAPITAL
Beijing

GOVERNMENT
One-party rule (China Communist Party) that allows some free market principles

DESCRIPTION OF FLAG
Red background with five yellow stars in the top left-hand corner

NATIONAL ANTHEM
Yi Yong Jun Jin Xing Qu (March of the Volunteers)

POPULATION
1.3 billion (2001)

LIFE EXPECTANCY
70 years

ETHNIC GROUPS
Han Chinese 92 percent; minorities 8 percent

OFFICIAL RELIGIONS
Buddhism 8 percent, Taoism 2.6 percent, Islam 1.4 percent, Protestantism 2 percent, Catholicism 1 percent (official 1997 estimates of 15 percent of religious believers of various faiths)

LITERACY RATE
81.5 percent of those aged 15 and above (1995)

OFFICIAL LANGUAGE
Putonghua (Mandarin)

TIME
Greenwich Mean Time plus 8 hours (GMT+0800)

WORK HOURS
The average worker works eight hours a day five days a week.

NATIONAL HOLIDAYS
New Year's Day (January 1), Spring Festival (January or February), Labor Day (May 1), National Day (October 1)

LEADERS IN LITERATURE
Zhang Kangkang—national prizes in China; first published work *The Dividing Line* (1975)
Gao Xingjian—2000 Nobel Prize/*Soul Mountain*
Ha Jin—1999 U.S. National Book Award/*Waiting*
Bei Dao—leading contemporary poet in China; American Academy of Arts and Letters member

LEADERS IN SPORT
Fu Mingxia—diving; 2000 Olympic gold medal
Deng Yaping—table tennis; world number one 1993–98
Wang Zhizhi—basketball; China's biggest star and first Asian in NBA; plays for Dallas Mavericks
Fang Zhiyi—China soccer team captain; plays in English league for Crystal Palace
Ma Junren—China's coach of world-class athletes dubbed as "Ma's Army"

TIME LINE

IN CHINA	IN THE WORLD

2205–1766 B.C.
Xia Dynasty

1766–1123 B.C.
Shang Dynasty

1122–221 B.C.
Zhou Dynasty

753 B.C.
Rome is founded.

221–206 B.C.
First emperor Qin Shihuang unites China;
construction of the Great Wall is completed.

116–17 B.C.
The Roman Empire reaches its greatest extent
under Emperor Trajan (98–17 B.C.).

A.D. 24
Invention of paper

A.D. 150
Buddhism is introduced from India.

A.D. 600
Height of Mayan civilization

1000
The Chinese perfect gunpowder
and begin to use it in warfare.

1300
Construction of the Grand Canal is completed.

1530
Beginning of trans-Atlantic slave trade organized by
Portuguese in Africa

1558–1603
Reign of Elizabeth I of England

1620
Pilgrim Fathers sail the Mayflower to America.

1644–1911
Qing Dynasty

1776
U.S. Declaration of Independence

1789–99
The French Revolution

1839–64
The Chinese are defeated in the Opium Wars
and forced to open some ports to trade;
Hong Kong is ceded to Britain.

1861
U.S. Civil War begins.

IN CHINA	IN THE WORLD
	1869 The Suez Canal is opened.
1911 Sun Yat-sen establishes the Republic.	
	1914 World War I begins.
1919 May Fourth Movement	
1921 Chinese Communist Party is founded.	
1925 Sun Yat-sen dies; Chiang Kai-shek succeeds and heads the Nationalists.	
1934–35 The Long March	
1937 Outbreak of Sino-Japanese War	
	1939 World War II begins.
	1945 The United States drops atomic bombs on Hiroshima and Nagasaki.
1949 The People's Republic of China is founded; Chiang's forces escape to Taiwan.	**1949** North Atlantic Treaty Organization (NATO) is formed.
	1957 Russians launch Sputnik.
1958 The Great Leap Forward	
1966–69 The Cultural Revolution	**1969** First man on the moon
1976 Zhou Enlai and Mao Zedong die.	
1979 Deng Xiaoping implements economic reforms.	
	1986 Nuclear power disaster at Chernobyl in Ukraine
1989 Army quashes student demonstrations at Tiananmen Square; many students are killed. Jiang Zemin comes to power.	**1991** Break-up of Soviet Union
1997 Deng Xiaoping dies; Hong Kong is returned to China.	**2001** World population surpasses 6 billion.

GLOSSARY

fan ("fun")
Cooked rice

feng shui ("fehng shu-ay")
The art of living in harmony with the physical environment so as to attract good fortune

Guan Yin ("Kwahn-yin")
Chinese Goddess of Mercy

guanxi ("KWAHNG-see")
Interpersonal relationships that benefit the parties involved through the exchange of favors

Han
China's ethnic majority

hao ("how")
Good, enjoyable

Hua Qiao ("hu-ah chi-ow")
Overseas Chinese

jiaozi ("chi-ao zher")
Crescent-shaped dumplings filled with meat and vegetables

laoshi ("LA-OW sheh")
A term of respect meaning "teacher"

mien ("me-an")
Noodles

pinyin ("pin-yin")
A system of writing Chinese words in the English alphabet

Putonghua
China's official language, also known as Mandarin

qi ("chi")
The energy or force that flows through all living things

qigong ("chi-kong")
A martial art practiced as a form of therapeutic exercise

taijiquan ("tie-chi-chwaan")
Chinese shadow boxing

weiqi ("way-chee")
Chinese board game played with black and white markers. *Wei* means "to surround" while *qi* means "board game".

wushu ("woo-shoo")
A collective name for different forms of Chinese martial arts, the most popular being Chinese boxing (as seen in *kung fu* movies where hands and legs move lightning fast, with long, high jumps)

xian sheng ("si-anh shehng")
A term of address meaning "Mr." For example, Mao Zedong Xian Sheng means Mr. Mao Zedong.

yang ("young")
The active life force or energy. *Yang* is masculinity, sun, heat, and fire.

yin ("yin")
The passive life force or energy. *Yin* is represented by femininity, darkness, cold, and water.

FURTHER INFORMATION

BOOKS

Barnhart, Richard M., et. al. *Three Thousand Years of Chinese Painting*. New York: Yale University Press, 1997.

Chang, Jung. *Wild Swans: Three Daughters of China*. New York: Vintage Anchor Publishing, 1992.

Fairbank, John King and Merle Goldman. *China: A New History*. London: Harvard University Press, 1998.

Liou, Caroline, et. al. *Lonely Planet China*. 7th edition. London: Lonely Planet Publications, 2000.

Salisbury, Harrison E. *The New Emperors*. London: HarperCollins Publishers, 1993.

Sinclair, Kevin and Iris Wong Po-yee. *Culture Shock! China*. Oregon: Graphic Arts Center Publishing Company, 2002.

Taylor, Chris, et. al. *China*. Melbourne: Lonely Planet Publications, 1996.

WEBSITES

China Daily. www.chinadaily.com.cn

China Internet Information Centre. www.china.org.cn

Consulate-General of the People's Republic of China in New York.
    www.nyconsulate.prchina.org/eng/index.html

International Institute for Applied Systems Analysis (link to China). www.iiasa.ac.at

Ministry of Foreign Trade and Economic Cooperation. www.moftec.gov.cn

Ministry of Railways. www.chinamor.cn.net

Population Reference Bureau (link to China). www.prb.org

People's Daily. www.people.com.cn

PlanetArk (link to China). www.planetark.org

State Economic and Trade Commission. www.setc.gov.cn

State Statistics Bureau, China. www.stats.gov.cn

The World Bank Group (type "China" in the search box). www.worldbank.org

VIDEOS/DVDs

China: A Century of Revolution. Winstar Home Entertainment, 2002.

Empire of the Sun. Warner Studios, 2001. Theatrical release 1987.

The Last Emperor. Artisan Entertainment, 2002. Theatrical release 1987.

Touring China. Questar Inc., 1998.

MUSIC

Chinese Piano Concertos. ASV Living Era, 1998.

Classical Chinese Folk Music. Arc Music, 2000.

Masterpieces of Chinese Traditional Music. Wind Records, 2000.

BIBLIOGRAPHY

Carter, Alden. *Modern China*. New York: Franklin Watts, 1986.
Minford, John (translator). *Favourite Folktales of China*. Beijing: New World Press, 1983.
Miyazima, Yashukiko. *Children of the World: China*. Milwaukee, WI: Gareth Stevens, 1988.
Rau, Margaret. *Holding up the Sky: Young People in China*. New York: Lodestar Books, 1983.
Wei Jinzhi. *100 Allegorical Tales from Traditional China*. Hong Kong: Joint Publications, 1982.
Wood, Frances. *People at Work in China*. New York: David and Charles, 1988.

INDEX